C000246496

A HORSE IS A HORSE OF COURSE:

HORSE BEHAVIOUR EXPLAINED

OR

WHAT YOU *REALLY* NEED TO KNOW ABOUT HORSES SO THAT YOU DON'T MAKE MISTAKES

JANE MYERS AND STUART MYERS
EQUICULTURE PUBLISHING

Disclaimer

About this book

This book is part of the Equiculture Sustainable Horsekeeping Series.

Understanding horse behaviour is a very important part of caring for horses properly. It is very easy to convince yourself that your horse is content to do all of the things that you enjoy, but a better approach is to understand that your horse sees the world quite differently to you, after all, you are a primate (hunter/gatherer) and your horse is a very large hairy herbivore! So it's not surprising that you both have a very different view of the world.

We recommend that if in doubt take everything 'back to basics' and think about what a horse has evolved to be. This book describes horse behaviour in both the wild 'natural' environment and in the domestic environment. It then looks at how you can reduce stress in the domestic horse by understanding and acknowledging their real needs, resulting in a more 'well-adjusted', content and thriving animal.

Do your horse a favour and read this book!

Thank you for buying this book and please consider either leaving a review or contacting us with feedback, stuart@equiculture.com.au.

About the authors

Jane Myers MSc (Equine Science) is the author of several professional books about horses including the best selling book Managing Horses on Small Properties (published by CSIRO). Jane is particularly interested in sustainable horsekeeping practices and issues, such as low stress horse management that also delivers environmental benefits. Jane has lived and breathed horses from a young age and considers herself to be very fortunate in that she has been able to spend her life riding, training and studying these amazing animals.

Stuart Myers (BSc) has a background in human behaviour and has been a horse husband for more years than he cares to remember.

Stuart and Jane present workshops to horse owners in Australia, the USA and the UK about sustainable horse and horse property management as part of their business, Equiculture.

See the Equiculture website www.equiculture.com.au where you will find lots of great information about horsekeeping and please join the mailing list while you are there!

Jane and Stuart also have another website that supports their Horse Rider's Mechanic series of workbooks (1, 2 and 3). This website is www.horseridersmechanic.com why not have a look?

Contents

A horse is a horse of course

Understanding horse characteristics is a very important part of horse ownership. By reading this book you will learn about what it really means to be a horse and how by understanding and utilising this knowledge it is possible to improve the health and welfare of your horse.

What horses are...

This section looks at why horses are built the way they are, their physiology, and how the physiological characteristics of horses are linked to their behaviour, just as they are with all animals including humans.

Horses are part of the equine family which also includes asses (donkeys) and zebra (and of course ponies which for the sake of clarity will be encompassed with horses in this book). The equine family used to be much larger but many species of equine are now extinct.

Domestic horses are part of the equine family which includes donkeys and zebra.

Equus ferus caballus is the scientific name for domestic horses. They can usually produce offspring with other members of the equine family (such as a horse/donkey cross which results in a mule) but any resulting offspring are *usually* unable to reproduce (are sterile). In their natural environment, equines were/are hunted by predators such as large felines and canines although in modern times many of their natural predators have also become extinct.

These horses are doing 'what comes naturally' to any grazing herbivore. Grazing is the most important behaviour that horses carry out. Horses spend (or should spend) more time grazing than all of their other behaviours put together.

Horses are *herbivores* (plant/herbage eaters). There are three main types of herbivore, ruminants, pseudo-ruminants and non-ruminants:

- The ruminant group includes animals such as cows, sheep, goats, yak, buffalo, moose and other animals such as bison, gazelle, antelope, deer and giraffe.

- The pseudo-ruminant group are camelids, i.e. camels, alpacas and llamas.

- The non-ruminant group includes all *equines*, but also rhinoceros and tapirs, which are the only living relatives of the equine family. Elephants are also non-ruminants.

Humans, pigs and dogs are also non-ruminants but they are *omnivore* which means that they usually eat meat *and* plants.

Your horse is more closely related to tapirs and rhinoceros than to sheep and cows.

Ruminants and non-ruminant grazing *herbivores* (apart from elephants) are all part of the group of animals called *ungulates*, which simply means hoofed mammals (pigs are ungulates too despite being omnivores), however there are many important differences between ruminants and non-ruminants despite them both belonging to the *ungulate* group. It is important to understand the differences between the two animal types because it is often presumed that all grazing animals have the same or similar needs which can lead to management and welfare issues.

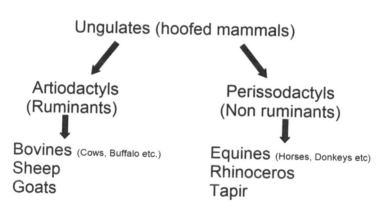

Ungulates (hoofed mammals)

Artiodactyls
(Ruminants)

Perissodactyls
(Non ruminants)

Bovines (Cows, Buffalo etc.)
Sheep
Goats

Equines (Horses, Donkeys etc)
Rhinoceros
Tapir

The main differences are in the feet and in the digestive systems but also in behaviour. Ruminants such as cows and sheep etc. are 'even toed ungulates' (*artiodactyla*) because the line of symmetry in the foot goes between the second and third toes. Non-ruminants (i.e. equines, rhinoceros and tapirs) are 'odd toed ungulates' (*perissodactyla*) as the line of symmetry in the foot goes through the middle of the third toe. In equines only the third toe remains, the others have almost disappeared through the process of evolution (the 'splint' bones at the side of the cannon bones are all that remains of the second and fourth toes).

It is the differences in the digestive systems (which also results in differences in behaviour) that are particularly important. Ruminants (such as cows and sheep) have a *rumen*. This is a large area that is positioned *before* the intestines and this is where they carry out much of their digestion. Therefore another name for ruminants is *foregut fermenters*. Ruminants initially chew and swallow their food more quickly than equines because they regurgitate it later to 're chew' it more thoroughly (sometimes called 'chewing the cud'). Non-ruminants (such as equines) do not have a rumen and carry out most of their digestion in their intestines (after the stomach) hence equines are called *hindgut fermenters*.

*The line of symmetry in the foot goes **between** the middle digits in animals such as pigs and cows and **through** the middle digit in animals such as rhinoceros and horses.*

Pig   Rhinoceros   Cow   Horse

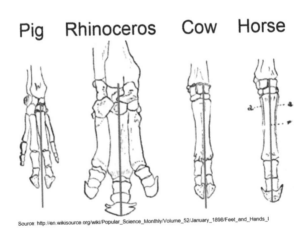

Source: http://en.wikisource.org/wiki/Popular_Science_Monthly/Volume_52/January_1898/Feet_and_Hands_I

Fermentation is *very* important to *all* herbivores. Plant material is impossible to digest in the same way that carnivores (animals, such

4

as cats, that eat only meat) and omnivores digest meat and certain other food types (meat eaters mainly use digestive juices that are rich in enzymes to digest their food). Grass plants in particular are coated with a very tough substance called cellulose. Herbivores require assistance to break down this cellulose, therefore animals that predominantly eat plants have to host (provide a home for) large numbers of micro-organisms (sometimes called 'friendly bugs') that will break the cellulose down for them in to a form that they can then digest.

These micro-organisms in the gut are so important that without them a horse cannot survive. When you feed a horse you are actually feeding billions of micro-organisms that in turn feed your horse. This is a good example of what is termed a 'symbiotic relationship' because each organism needs the other for survival.

What is regarded as the leg and hoof of a horse (from below the 'knee' or hock) is actually the same as the middle toe or finger, and its fingernail or toenail, on a primate (such as us). The joint on the front leg of a horse that is commonly called the 'knee' is the same joint as our wrist (carpus) and the joint on the hind leg of a horse called the hock is the same as our ankle (tarsus).

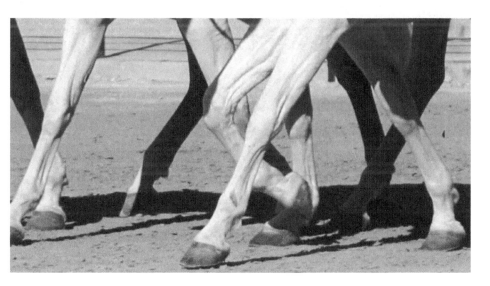

Therefore, ruminants (such as cows and sheep) host these micro organisms mainly in the foregut and non-ruminants (such as horses) host these micro-organisms mainly in the hindgut. Horses have a very large *caecum* (which is the same organ as the human appendix but relatively much larger and more important to the animal) and a *huge* large intestine (LA). The caecum and LA are where the greatest numbers of these very important micro-organisms ('friendly bugs') live. Omnivores (such as humans and dogs) also provide a home in their gut for beneficial micro-organisms that help them with the digestion of plants. However these micro-organisms are not *as* crucial to them because omnivores eat other types of food as well (such as meat/fish etc.).

There are many important differences between horses and ruminants (such as cows). In particular they differ in their behaviour and in the way that they digest their food. This horse is doing its job of 'standing guard' over its only companion, a cow, while the cow lies down. The cow does not take its turn and 'stand guard' over the horse when the horse lies down because cows do not do this! An example of why animals need their own kind as companions (although in this case it is better than no companion) because different species have different behaviours.

The mouth parts of cows and horses also differ significantly. Horses have six upper and six lower incisor teeth which meet edge to edge. This means that they can clip grass and other plants *very* close to the ground. They also have a highly mobile (prehensile) top lip which allows them to be extremely selective when they are grazing. Cows have only lower incisors (of which there are eight) and their top lip is not very mobile at all, instead a cow's tongue is highly mobile (prehensile). Cows have to rely on their tongue to break the grass and so cannot eat very short grass. Sheep and goats also have mobile lips (like horses) and are also able to eat very close to the ground. This ability of a horse to eat very short grass is beneficial in the wild where forage may be difficult to obtain at times, but can work against your horse (and your land) in the domestic situation because it leads to overgrazing if you do not manage your pasture properly.

Horses have six upper and six lower incisors which meet edge to edge, like a pair of scissors in the mouth!

Horses are highly successful as wild and feral animals in various climates around the world. Two of the reasons that horses are able to survive in very harsh conditions are due to this ability to eat very short grass (therefore, if necessary, they can eat what other animals leave behind) *and* they do not need to 're-chew' (ruminate) their food (which takes time and energy). Horses can increase the amount they eat, even if this food is very low in energy, by increasing the amount of time they spend eating (up to 20 hours a day if necessary). Ruminants take time to extract the maximum amount of nutrition out of every mouthful, whereas horses rely on maximising their intake instead.

Another very important fact about horses is that gastric acid is made and secreted into the stomach continuously (rather than just as a meal is eaten which is the case with most omnivores). A free living horse has access to fibre most if not all of the time (even when this fibre is very poor quality and low in energy, such as leaves and even twigs). This means that a free-living horse can nearly always find something fibrous to eat and so the acid in the stomach is usually buffered by the saliva that the horse swallows while chewing. If domestic horses do not have access to enough fibre (and therefore they are not chewing and swallowing enough saliva) this acid reaches critical levels in the stomach and causes *gastric ulcers*. Gastric ulcers are a *very* common occurrence in domestic horses due to the way that these horses are usually managed (on a diet that is too low in fibre). Not getting enough fibre is also a reason why domestic horses will sometimes eat poisonous plants, strip the bark from trees or chew fences. Indeed horses will eat almost anything rather than allow painful gastric acid to build up in their stomach. For this reason 'starving' even a fat horse is not the right way to go about managing weight (more about this later).

Domestic horses range in size far more than their more natural living counterparts. Wild and feral horses are usually between 12hh (hh = 'hands high') and 15hh but are most commonly around 14hh.

One 'hand' equals four inches or approximately 10 cm. The use of the 'hand' is an ancient but still widely used way of measuring horses from the wither (top of the shoulders) to the ground.

Domestic horses have been manipulated (by breeding) to range in size from less than 8hh to more than 20hh. Apart from size however, free-living *and* domestic horses share the same the physiological and behavioural characteristics.

Horses have *very* sensitive skin which is necessary for detecting flying pests and parasites. In the free-living situation some species of insects suck blood and will seriously debilitate a horse over time. Horses can 'twitch' their skin in many areas of the body and will stamp a front leg or even kick forward with a back leg at their belly if they feel the light touch of an insect or what they perceive to be an insect (so be careful to touch a horse firmly otherwise it may think an insect has landed on its' skin).

Domestic horses have a larger size range than their more natural living counterparts but they all share the same physiological and behavioural characteristics.

Some parts of the horse are even more sensitive than others and these include the top lip, muzzle, flanks, eyes, ears, feet and legs. The top lip has many nerve endings and, as already mentioned, is highly mobile (prehensile) which allows a horse to select certain plants. The muzzle is covered in whiskers that help a horse to 'feel' in much the same way as a cat uses its' whiskers to 'feel'. These whiskers should never be removed (but in the case of domestic horses often are). The flanks are sensitive to the extent of being very ticklish in some horses. The eyes, ears, feet and legs are essential to wild horse survival therefore a horse that is not accustomed to being handled by humans is particularly wary of these areas being touched.

The relatively large eyes of a horse are situated on the *sides* of the head which gives excellent all round vision at the expense of sharp forward focusing vision. In effect, a horse has a much wider peripheral vision and can see much further than we can, but has a smaller focal point. Horses are unable to focus on objects at the same speed that we can and this lack of sharp focusing can cause a horse to be anxious about an object until the object has been properly identified. If horses cannot ascertain what a potentially scary object is very quickly then they prepare for flight because in the wild spending time thinking about what to do next could lead to being caught and eaten.

The eyes of a horse are situated high on the head so that they can see predators approaching while grazing. This also reduces the amount of grass seeds that get into the eyes.

By contrast a horse can detect moving objects in the distance that a human eye would struggle to see. Horses also notice when *unfamil-*

iar objects are positioned in a *familiar* place because they take the *whole* situation into account when looking for potential dangers.

A horse's eyes are situated a long way from the mouth in order to lift the eyes out of the grass when grazing and increase vision. This also has the advantage of reducing the amount of grass seeds that get into the eyes (a potentially dangerous occurrence for a horse).

When the head is in the grazing position a horse can see along either side of its' legs. At all times a horse has a small blind spot directly in front of the face (between the eyes) and is unable to see the area below and behind the chin.

Having a long neck allows a horse to see directly behind and directly in front with only small movements of the head. If a horse becomes aware of a possible danger the head is immediately raised above the level of the body where all round vision is easily possible. The only time a horse is unable to see behind their body is when the head is straight forward and level with the body (the usual position of the head when being ridden).

The positioning of the eyes on the side of the head means that the horse has excellent all round vision. Grazing herbivores tend to all share this characteristic whereas predators (such as ourselves, cats and dogs), have their eyes positioned facing forwards.

In addition to raising the head for better vision, the long neck allows a horse to easily reach the ground to graze, but also acts as a balance for the body while moving at speed. Yet another function of the long neck is to permit the head to swing from side to side to bite at flies on the body or to reach out to nip/bite another horse. The teeth are sharp and the jaws are extremely strong (because a horse spends so much time biting plants and chewing). A bite from a horse causes a crushing rather than a tearing injury (as is the case with a cat or dog bite). Horses nip or bite each other when playing or asserting themselves, but they also use their front teeth (incisors) to mutually groom one another, an essential bonding behaviour among horses.

The ears of a horse are situated right on top of their head and are serviced by numerous muscles (in us most of these muscles have disappeared through the process of evolution). These muscles enable each ear to swivel 180 degrees providing the horse with potentially 360 degrees of hearing without even having to move the head. The ears also work independently so that a horse can have one ear facing forward and one back at the same time, or one ear 'fixed' on something and the other 'ranging' and searching for other sounds. The possibilities are endless. This gives a horse the ability to hear very well indeed, so a horse can hear objects approaching well before we humans can. The ears serve the dual function of being used for hearing *and* for signaling certain behaviours as part of the body language of horses.

This horse is using one ear to listen behind as he also looks and listens forward. A horse's long neck has various functions including lifting the head above the body for all round vision and hearing.

The hoof of a horse is relatively very small and lightweight (compare it to a human foot) on the end of a leg that is concertinaed (the joints are always partially bent when the horse is standing or moving slowly) which allows a lot of extension when running and kicking. This means that very little energy is required to move the hoof and it can move very quickly, it also means that a horse can kick with accuracy, speed and strength if required. If a horse is being attacked by a predator it can defend itself by kicking backwards *and* running away at the same time. This relatively lightweight hoof has a small area of contact (like stiletto heels on a soft floor) it is capable of causing a lot of damage to potential predators.

A horse is also capable of striking forward with a front leg if necessary. In the free-living situation a horse that is surrounded by predators will strike at them with a front leg or even rear to use both front legs to strike and stamp if they cannot get away.

The hoof of a horse is relatively very small and lightweight on the end of a leg that is built to have maximum extension. Horses can kick with speed and accuracy.

Horses have a strong sense of smell. As well as being necessary for food selection, a horse uses this sense of smell when assessing a potentially dangerous situation. Many horses are unsettled in windy weather and one reason for this is thought to be because wind distorts and adds to the normal noise level making it more difficult for a horse to hear potential danger. The wind also brings various scents that a horse then has to decipher.

Horses do not like wind and rain together and will turn their rump into the wind and rain to protect their head. Turning their rump in this way causes the tail to 'fan out' across their rump which helps to keep the hairless areas directly under the tail warm and dry. At the same time the wind blows the rest of the tail between the back legs to help protect the hairless areas between the back legs (the udder of a female and sheath of a male horse) and the belly. For this reason the tail of a domestic horse that 'lives out', like the whiskers, should not be cut (except to shorten it slightly if it grows long enough to drag on the ground).

The whiskers of a domestic horse should never be removed (but often are). A horse needs these whiskers to 'feel' with, in much the same way as a cat.

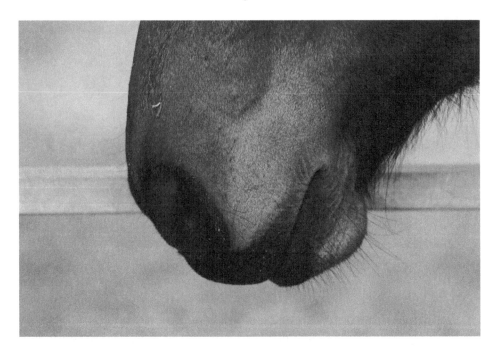

The long forelock and mane of a horse is there to protect the head and neck from rain and from flies. They also help to keep these parts of the body warm when necessary so again they should always be left intact in a horse that spends time outdoors.

Horses have very large lungs which enable them to accelerate from slowly walking and grazing to moving very quickly indeed if and when necessary. This can be achieved at just a moment's notice. Horses are also able to keep up speed for relatively long distances. In comparison to a cheetah for example, which is *extremely* fast but can only run at high speed for very short distances, a healthy horse can sprint fast enough to get away from most predators *and* keep up a reasonable level of speed for hours if necessary. Therefore horses are supreme grazing athletes in many respects.

Horses are supreme grazing athletes in many respects. Healthy horses will run around on a fairly regular basis if given the opportunity.

The way that horses are built, their physiology, is closely linked to their behaviour, and in turn is vital for their survival. Everything about horses, including their large eyes, long legs, sensitive skin and all of the other things that make horses what they are, has evolved for a purpose. That purpose is to thrive in a range of climates and landscapes throughout the world as a free-living, grazing, herd animal.

What horses are not...

As humans it is very easy to assume that animals 'are just like us' and that they want the same things that we do. Domestic horses have no input into who owns them, how they are kept and what their owners do to them therefore it is very important that we *understand* what is important to them (and what is not) so that we can continually strive to improve the way that we keep them.

It is commonly regarded as 'normal' and 'good horse care' for a horse to be permanently separated from other horses. It is also common for domestic horses to stand around for many hours a day with nothing to do and not enough fibre to eat. These and other practices have become normalised in the horse world and this is a very sad situation for the domestic horse.

Horses are large grazing herbivores and are meant to eat grass and a variety of other plants. They are also meant to live as part of a herd and move around for many hours a day.

We have established that horses are large grazing herbivores and that they are not ruminants, like cows or sheep. But there are other important facts that we need to acknowledge about horses and how we interact with them. It is important *not* to label horses (or any animals for that matter) with human characteristics (to anthropomorphise) but instead to try to view their behaviour from their perspective. It is a curious human characteristic to look for human behavioural traits in many things ranging from inanimate objects such as their car to animate creatures such as their pets and other animals. Humans then use this misinformation as a reason for treating these objects or creatures in a certain way. This is not usually done with any malicious intent, quite the opposite in fact, but the problem is that while it can be fun for humans to anthropomorphise (and harmless in the case of inanimate objects such as their car) it is not helpful and can actually be harmful because it disregards an animal's real needs and replaces them with human needs.

We tend to think that horses have the same needs as we do. This horse is stabled full time and the mark on the wall is due to a stereotypic behaviour (head swinging).

Beware of attaching human emotions and needs to horses as this may impede understanding of their true behaviour and can even lead to welfare issues. For example, contrary to popular opinion, horses do not bear grudges (a common human failing!). They do not sulk if they cannot 'have their own way' (another common human failing!). There is no proof that horses see us as they would see another horse (it is highly unlikely in fact because we look nothing like a horse!) so acting like an 'alpha mare' is not likely to get your horse's 'respect' (only fear if you insist on trying to dominate your horse). Another common misconception about horses is that they deliberately set out to upset or even hurt you. This is why horses are often labelled with descriptions such as 'lazy', 'mean' or even 'cunning'. Likewise it is common to hear horse people say that a horse 'knows he is doing wrong' when in fact horses are horses and have no concept of what we humans regard as 'right' and 'wrong'.

Another example is that we might think that a horse 'needs' a warm stable and/or lots of rugs because as humans that is what we tend to value highly, albeit human versions i.e. a warm house and clothes. But horses usually place a higher value on other things instead. They value freedom to move, the companionship of other equines and high fibre foodstuffs. Horses do need shade (in hot weather) and shelter (in bad weather) however it is best if a horse can choose when to access these resources rather than having them forced upon them as they so often are in the domestic situation.

Horses need high fibre foodstuffs and they need the companionship of other horses. They also need movement and lots of it. Horses do not move because they know they need to 'keep fit' they move because they have an innate need to move, a subtle but important difference.

18

Another example is that we humans often value (in ourselves and others) such behaviours as risk taking (for thrills and 'personal development'), education (in order to 'better ourselves') and exercise (because we know we should). Horses have no concept of 'personal development'. They do not strive to challenge themselves because it will 'do them good', in fact they resist taking risks 'just for the fun of it' (as we do). They do not exercise themselves to 'keep fit', they move because they have an innate *need* to move.

There are many other important differences between humans and horses. Humans are by nature one of the top predators (hunters) on earth whereas horses are hunted by predators (carnivores and omnivores). These differences often lead to a lack of understanding because as predators we tend to think a certain way whereas our horses think quite differently! It is a good idea to keep reminding yourself that you are the one with the plan, the agenda; the domestic horse is just trying to figure out which behaviours will help them to survive and thrive.

Beliefs about modern horsekeeping is an assortment of ideas, superstitions etc. from a time when horses were kept for a purpose (for work) combined with now when horses are kept mainly (in the western world) for recreation. If you are struggling to understand what you need to do in order to improve the welfare of your horse always try to think about what the basic requirements are for a horse. Free-living (wild/feral) equines usually have access to the things that they need to survive and thrive. Many domestic horses do not and this can lead to welfare issues. All of these important needs and how you can provide them will be covered in more detail throughout the rest of this book.

Acknowledging that horses are not like humans does not mean that we should disregard or even say that horses do not have emotions, feelings etc. Horses are a complex animal that have intricate needs. As humans we should strive to understand what is really important to horses rather than simply assume that they want what we do. This means that we have to learn about horse behaviour.

Horse behaviour and 'lifestyle'

We owe it to our domestic horses to understand and acknowledge their behaviour properly. In order to learn how a domestic horse *should* behave we actually need to start with learning about the behaviour of free-living horses. We cannot surmise what is normal horse behaviour by watching domestic horses, because domestic horses have to modify their behaviour due to man-made constraints such as fences, feed times and so on. In a natural setting horses carry out behaviours without being hampered by such constraints.

Free-living equines such as these Konik ponies have a rich and varied 'lifestyle'. These particular ponies are part of a grazing project in the UK that aims to recreate bio-diverse (multi species) grassland from land that was previously farmland.

There is a lot of information available about how horse behaviour relates to training but not as much information is available about how horse behaviour relates to their management. In fact the horse world is not even so forward thinking as many modern zoos in numerous respects and 'tradition' plays a part in holding back change. Much of the available information about horse management is based on outdated beliefs and practices that came about long before the behaviour and physiology of horses were researched scientifically. This traditional information tends to focus predominantly on the needs and conveniences of humans and not horses. Despite relatively recent research findings that disprove much of this outdated information about horses, old beliefs are still unfortunately entrenched in the 'culture' of the horse world.

From various scientific studies we know how equines behave when living wild or feral (escaped/released into a free-living situation). We also know that domestic horses retain their 'wild' characteristics because in cases where they have been released or have escaped (for example Mustangs in the USA and Brumbies in Australia) they have survived and thrived. This tells us that they still possess their natural behaviours. We also know that when animals are prevented from carrying out their natural behaviours they can become stressed and this affects their behaviour and health. All animals, including zoo animals, domestic animals and humans, develop behavioural and physiological problems if their 'lifestyle' is inadequate and prevents them from carrying out basic but fundamental behaviours.

Ignoring an animal's real needs can result in the development of stereotypic behaviours such as 'crib biting'. Species specific variations of these behaviours are often seen in zoo animals, domestic animals and humans.

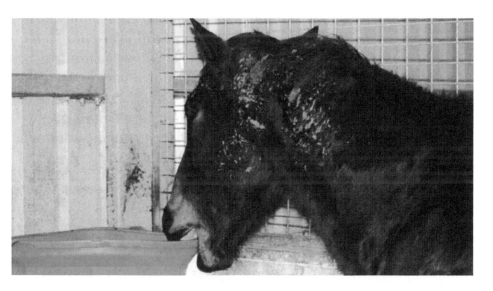

Stereotypic behaviours are common in domestic horses and are unfortunately termed 'vices' in the horse world (see the section **Abnormal horse behaviour**). These behaviours are never seen in free-living horses. So we have to ask the question, what is happening to domestic horses to cause them to develop these stress related behavioural conditions?

When compared to free-living horses, domestic horses generally live longer, but there is an ever increasing rise in dietary and age related problems such as obesity, laminitis (a very painful and possibly life threatening condition of the hooves) and insulin resistance etc. Gastric ulcers and colic are also very common in domestic horses, with colic being an especially dangerous condition. Again, what can we learn from free-living horses which will enable domestic horses to live healthier lives?

Domestic horses and wild/feral horses have the same behavioural characteristics. Their behaviour is governed by innate instincts (behaviour that is natural to them) that drives them to behave a certain way, sometimes in a way that seems illogical to us as humans.

When we understand what is important to horses we can aim to keep them in a way that mimics their natural environment as much as possible. Domestic horses cannot usually be kept in a way that completely mimics natural living because the natural 'lifestyle' of a horse involves living with access to very large areas of land, usually thousands of acres. It is possible however to strike a very good compromise when the important details are understood, and that is what we should strive to do if we are to be responsible horse owners.

Natural living horses

Additional factors to some of the already mentioned points about natural living (wild/feral) horses result in them having a very different 'lifestyle' to domestic horses. To summarise the 'lifestyle' of natural living horses:

- Natural living horses usually live in a family group, a band or small herd, consisting of a stallion, a few mares and their offspring. Occasionally multi-male bands (with females) are formed. The offspring (fillies and colts) generally leave the family band when they are around two years old (colts usually sooner than fillies) and they join other bands (fillies) or form 'bachelor groups' (colts) where they live until they form a breeding unit with a filly or win a group of mares (or gather some ousted fillies) of their own. Some of these colts and stallions never actually win/gather their own group of fillies/mares and spend their life in a group with other bachelor stallions. These bands, bachelor groups etc. may intermingle, coming together to form a larger herd for part of the day and branch off at other times. It all depends on the terrain, climate, feed availability etc.

- Natural living horses may 'pair bond' with another horse in the group that is similar in age, size and sex. These bonds are often for life.

- Natural living horses are on the alert for many hours a day, although this behaviour is shared with other members of the herd (one of the most important reasons that grazing animals live in herds, otherwise they would have to be permanently vigilant and would eventually become exhausted). Even when not particularly alert they are able to become alert very quickly and react with lightning speed to danger if necessary.

- Natural living horses eat a very high fibre/low sugar/low starch/low protein diet and graze/forage for between 12 and 20 hours a day (but generally around 14 to 16 hours). Grazing/foraging usually takes up more time than all of their other behaviours put together.

- Natural living horses travel large distances a day from feed to water in what is known as the 'home range' (a large area that contains the grazing/foraging/water/shelter that they need). Horses walk steadily while grazing and also have to travel between where water is and where feed is (the plants nearest the water are always the first to be eaten out). It depends on various factors but free-living horses often travel around 20 miles (32 km) a day and can travel a lot further if necessary. Again the distance travelled is highly dependent on feed availability. When moving around the home range the horses often travel in single file as the tracking makes it easier to travel over the terrain, however once they begin grazing the band spreads itself out, searching for and selecting different plant species.

- Natural living horses wear their hooves down by moving across a variety of terrains ranging from soft and wet to abrasive and dry. In addition to wearing their hooves their circulation benefits from all this movement. Contraction and expansion of the hooves as they leave the ground and touch down again helps to pump blood and lymphatic fluid around the body.

- Natural living horses cope with a variety of climates and changing seasons. In many countries free-living horses cope with climates that range from very cold and wet to very hot and dry and everything in between. They utilise their stores of body fat in hard times and utilise their thicker winter coat to protect them in extreme weather conditions. In hot weather horses use a lot of energy to cool themselves because their large body, although slow to heat up, takes a long time to cool down. Horses, like humans, use sweat to cool the body.

- Natural living horses reproduce regularly. Mares produce a foal most years or two out of every three years therefore mares are usually pregnant with another foal while feeding a current foal at foot. This foal will continue to drink from its dam until at least the next foal arrives a year later, sometimes the yearling continues to drink from its dam even while she is feeding a new foal (and is pregnant with the next). Youngsters are weaned gradually over an extended period. Milk production requires huge amounts of energy (which she can only get from eating as much as possible and using up stored body fat if necessary). Stallions work hard to keep their mares together and stay extra alert for any would be rivals of their band. Energy is also required to serve (mate) their mares when they are 'in season'.

- Natural living horses tend to have a shorter life span than domestic horses. This figure is somewhat skewed because most of the areas where horses live as wild or feral animals no longer contain predators but they still tend to live less time than domestic horses. In many cases natural living horses have a life span of around eight to ten years although the figure varies greatly from situation to situation as some free-living habitats are much milder than others in addition to having no predators.

Therefore natural living horses have lots of energy demands and have to work hard to meet these energy demands by eating as much as possible. Yet they have a low energy diet for much of the year, are constantly on the move, spend a lot of time alert and have to cope with temperature extremes and the demands of reproduction. We should also take into consideration that free-living horses manage all of this without help from humans in the form of 'wormers', rugs, farriers, dentists, stables, vets, supplementary feed etc.

In short natural living horses do many things throughout their day which results in a rich and varied 'lifestyle'. They also expend lots of energy in the process. This is very different to the average day in the life of a domestic horse.

Domestic horses

By contrast domestic horses are managed by humans for better or for worse; they have different stresses to their free-living counterparts. To summarise the 'lifestyle' of domestic horses:

- Domestic horses are often prevented from interacting with other horses; this can cause high levels of stress. Increasingly, besides being stabled separately, some horses are turned out separately. Being worked alone can also be stressful for a horse. Training can help to overcome this but the underlying innate need to be with other horses is still there.

Domestic horses are often kept alone and this can cause high levels of stress.

- Domestic horses are usually unable to select their own companions and any relationships they do make with other horses can be changed at any time.
- Domestic horses have no control over where they are at any point in their lives. They may be confined in a stable 24/7 or have 'free' access to grassy pasture, but their range is always restricted by walls or fences. They may be unable to get to higher/drier

ground if necessary so may be forced to stand for hours in muddy conditions when the weather is wet. Likewise if they are turned out in an area without shade/shelter they are unable to do anything about the situation if the weather is very hot or very poor. They are *totally reliant* on humans for water, food, shelter and shade.

- Domestic horses often have a diet that is inappropriately high in energy and too low in fibrous roughage. This results in a much shorter period of the day spent eating/chewing compared to the much longer grazing/chewing period of free-living horses. In fact many domestic horses spend less than three hours per day chewing compared to their wild/free-living counterparts who spend *at least* 12 hours per day chewing.

Horses are meant to spend many hours a day just chewing. Their jaws have evolved to work hard for hours at a time. Horses should preferably have access to ad-lib ('all you can eat') fibre.

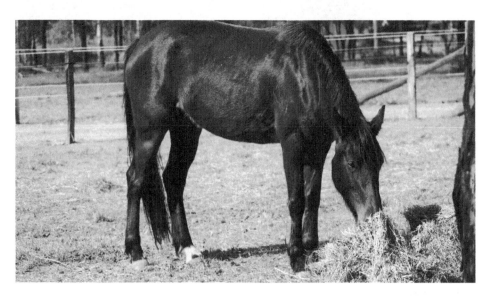

- Domestic horses may be forced to graze badly managed pasture that has high levels of parasitic 'worms' and contains many weeds and unsuitable grasses. Conversely domestic horses sometimes only have access to 'improved' grazing which contains plants that are too high in energy for most horses. The term 'improved' when applied to grasses and pasture means plants that have been developed (bred) for the much higher energy needs of beef and dairy cattle.

- Domestic horses often receive too little exercise and instead of having to find their own food it is given to them 'on a plate'. A domestic horse does not usually have to travel very far (sometimes not at all in the case of a fully stabled/yarded horse) during each day and night to graze and drink. This means that they miss out on the benefits of slow steady movement associated with grazing and traveling to a source of water.

- Domestic horses rarely get enough movement over a varied terrain to keep their hooves in good condition and have to rely on humans to keep their feet in good order, yet many domestic horses do not receive adequate hoof care.

- Domestic horses rarely have to deal with temperature extremes. Modern rugs and stables result in many domestic horses never experiencing the need to use energy to keep warm for example. Domestic horses are often inappropriately rugged and/or stabled, even when the weather is warm, causing stress.

Domestic horses do not usually have to travel very far to obtain their feed and they rarely have to deal with temperature extremes as they would in the wild. Many horses are over-rugged.

- Most domestic horses do not use energy for reproduction. This is just as well because there are already huge numbers of domestic *and* free-living equines in the world (about 43 million donkeys and 58 million horses worldwide according to Food and Agriculture Organization of the United Nations statistics). However, we need to remember that domestic horses do not have this natural drain on their energy and feed them accordingly.

- Domestic horses usually go through an unnatural weaning process which involves being separated from other horses when very young which is stressful in itself. Unnatural weaning is thought to lead to behavioural issues such as separation anxiety later in life.

- Domestic horses sometimes develop abnormal stereotypical behaviours not seen in natural living horses, this is usually due to inappropriate housing, management and feeding.

- Domestic horses tend to live for much longer than their wilder counterparts, regularly reaching their thirties and even forties. This means that there is now an increasingly ageing population of sedentary older horses.

As it can be seen, domestic horses have 'unnatural' stresses placed on them and usually have far less energy demands than free-living horses while at the same time receiving higher energy food. In fact many modern domestic horses have a 'lifestyle' that mirrors the lifestyle of many modern humans, not enough exercise and too much 'junk food'. So it is not surprising that domestic horses often have behavioural and obesity problems!

Communication

Herd animals need a way of communicating with one another so that they can live together in relative harmony. Horses use vocalisations and other noises but they also have a varied and complex repertoire of body language signals.

Vocalisations and other noises

Horses vocalise to signal various emotions and feelings, such as excitement, and when greeting one another. These are the main vocalisations and noises that horses make:

- Loud hard snort. Horses snort hard and loud when they are highly excited or sometimes when they are looking at something that they cannot immediately identify.

- Soft snort. Horses sometimes snort softly when in a situation where they are interested but less excited. Some horses make a snorting noise when cantering or galloping which is actually the vibration of the inner nostril.

- Roaring/whistling and other abnormalities. There are various abnormal noises that some horses make when they exert themselves. They are due to a (usually) congenital defect in the larynx and result in a horse not being able to breathe properly when working hard.

- Squeal. Horses squeal when greeting each other and when defending themselves, such as when kicking.

- Whinny. Horses make several noises ranging from a high pitched and urgent sounding whinny to a more relaxed greeting 'nicker'.

- Rumble. Horses make a low rumbling noise that is used as a greeting. This noise is commonly used by domestic horses when they see their owner approach with food.

- Nose blowing. Horses blow their nose when relaxed and to clear their airways. Horses have delicate lungs and need clean airways.

- Sigh. Horses sigh when relaxed. Horses hold their breath when very tense so a sigh is a sign that a horse has relaxed.

- Groan. When horses lie flat out on their side they sometimes groan because breathing can be difficult in this position.

When horses greet each other they often squeal while sniffing and blowing down their nostrils at each other.

Horses do not squeal or make any other vocalisation to signal pain (in the way that a dog yelps and whimpers when hurt for example). This is because a prey animal is usually unwilling to signal that they are in pain as this can mean that they will be seen, or more accurately heard, as being vulnerable and will be more likely to be singled out by a predator.

This fact also means that in the domestic situation horses are often perceived to be willing, happy, compliant etc. when in fact they might not be. If a domestic horse is in pain i.e. is lame or has been struck with a whip, the horse does not make a sound. This seemingly compliant behaviour extends to when a horse is stressed. Think about how dogs in cages (for example in an animal shelter) usually make it clear that they do not want to be there by barking, whining and by jumping up at the cage front. Overly confined (fully stabled for example) horses generally make no sound to signal that they would rather not be restrained and humans may take this to mean that the horse is 'happy' with the situation.

Body language

Different parts of a horse's body are used to communicate different signals:

- The ears of a horse are used in various ways to signal their intentions or state of mind. When a horse is very relaxed, such as when standing dozing, the ears also relax.

- An alert horse shows particularly strong body language. Generally speaking when a horse is alert the ears are 'pricked' (the ears are as far forward as they can go) and the head is held very high. The horse usually freezes because being still allows the horse to see and hear danger while being less noticeable to a potential predator. The horse may also emit a loud snort before attempting to spin and run away.

When a horse perceives danger they might initially 'freeze' because standing totally still allows them to see and hear better while at the same time being less noticeable to a potential predator.

- Both ears *pressed flat back* against the neck is usually a threat. Flat back ears are usually accompanied with wrinkling of the skin above the nostrils and sometimes below the eyes. This threat is commonly used between horses however it may also be used as a threat to humans/dogs etc. Just because a horse is threatening in this way does not mean that they are confident. Often when horses 'threaten' like this they are actually nervous and are hoping to frighten the object of their fear away.

This horse is laying her ears back at another horse but is actually nervous. She is behaving defensively because she is trapped in a small area with the other horse and if space allowed she would move away instead.

- Both ears pointing back but not pressed to the neck can mean that a horse is listening behind or that the horse is resting and has allowed the ears to relax. It is possible to tell the difference by looking further at the facial expression. If the horse is listening behind the expression on the face will be alert and the head will be held high. If the horse is dozing the eyes will also be half closed and the head will usually be lower. When riding it is possible to know what a horse is concentrating on by looking at the ears. Sometimes a horse will point one ear forward and one ear back to listen to the rider or to listen for anything coming up behind.

- The tail gives many signals. It is used to swish away flies and other insects but it is also swished when a horse is irritated. A horse 'clamps' the tail down (against the backside) when frightened and when about to kick or while actually kicking out. Sometimes a horse will also tuck the rump under when the tail is clamped. Clamping the tail and tucking the rump are an attempt to protect the reproductive organs from a kick.

This horse is actually listening behind rather than laying his ears back. Compare his expression with the previous picture.

- A relaxed horse will carry the tail slightly lifted when moving, without swishing (breeds such as Arabians naturally carry the tail higher than other breeds). If the horse is standing still the tail will be touching the body but relaxed (i.e. not clamped). An excited, exuberant horse will sometimes carry the tail up and over the back or straight up in the air like a flag.

- The muzzle, mouth, chin, eyes and nostrils give off many signs as to how a horse is feeling. The chin becomes 'bunched' and tight when a horse is tense/frightened. In addition the 'whites of the eyes' can be seen and the 'eyebrows' triangulate. The whole body can be tight and tense or soft and relaxed depending on how anxious or calm a horse is. The lower lip often droops when a horse is very relaxed or dozing. A young horse 'claps' the lips to older horses to signify youth. A horse 'curls' the top lip back when smelling something strange (called the Flehmen response). Stallions, some geldings and even some mares do this when sniffing a mare in season (oestrus) or sniffing the manure of other horses. Horses flare their nostrils and snort when alert.

An excited exuberant horse will sometimes carry the tail high in the air like a flag.

- A horse uses the head in a thrusting forward motion to drive another horse out of the way. A mare or stallion may direct other herd members in this way. Some horses, particularly stallions, swing the head around in a complete circle when feeling exuberant.

- A horse that is planning to kick may raise a back foot off the ground and hold it there as a threat. This will be accompanied by other body language signals such as ears laid flat back. A horse may also swing the back end towards the object in question, again initially as a threat.

- A horse that is 'resting a leg' is relaxed and may be dozing. However the 'resting a leg' stance can mean that a horse can pick up that leg to kick more quickly, so be careful when approaching a dozing horse. Always make sure that a dozing horse is aware that you are there by waiting until the horse has turned an ear or their head towards you before approaching, otherwise the horse can be startled and may kick out.

- Horses naturally lean into pressure rather than move away from pressure until they have been trained otherwise. When two horses kick each other they either press hard against each other or spring right away. This is because a kick is at its most dangerous a few feet away from a horse as the leg is fully extended at this point. Therefore the closer the horse is to the other horse, the less impact the strike will have (this is why people are taught that the safest way to pass behind a horse is to either move a long way out or put a hand on the rump and pass from one side to the other by moving very close against the horse).

It is through a combination of all these vocalisations and body language signals that horses communicate with each other when in a herd. Horses usually give many warning signals about their intentions before acting, although a nervous frightened horse will give less warning (and will quickly act defensively, especially if feeling trapped) than a more confident horse.

To the inexperienced horse person some of the more subtle expressions of this body language can be difficult to see, but any experienced person can easily read the body language of horses and does so without even having to think about it. It is up to you to learn how to read the signs. It is important to have a good understanding of how horses communicate so that you can take advantage of these warning signs and act accordingly.

Intelligence and learning ability

Measuring intelligence in animals is very difficult because as humans we tend to measure intelligence from a human perspective. Humans are *generally* able to be logical, are good problem solvers and are able to think things through. Humans and other predators needed these abilities to work as a team to outwit and catch varied and fast moving prey.

The brain of the horse is very different because horses do not have to catch prey and they have to be ready to run away from predators without having to stop and think about it. For example, when a lion or hyena is about to catch and eat you, stopping to think things through would lead to being caught and eaten!

Therefore horses and other prey animals have to be able to make instant snap decisions and flee very quickly if necessary. Additionally the staple foods of horses do not run away so they do not have to work out how to catch their dinner.

Horses have to make snap decisions about when to run and when not to. If in doubt they run anyway because in a natural situation a horse that spends time thinking about it and weighing up the odds would not survive.

Horses *are* very good at what is called 'trial and error' learning. A good example of trial and error learning is that of a horse that has learned to open gates. Sometimes a horse, while playing with a gate catch, will actually release it. Horses have a very tactile mouth; the top lip in particular is very mobile (prehensile), this means that a horse with nothing else to do will often 'fiddle' with objects such as gate catches (especially because the horse may spend many hours standing at a gate waiting to be fed). If the gate opens as a result of this fiddling the horse is immediately rewarded by being able to get to fresh grass outside the gate or by being able to move closer to where the supplementary feed comes from. The horse did not originally set out to open the gate however that was the result. The horse learns by *trial and error* that to fiddle with objects (such as gate catches) can lead to a reward and is therefore more likely to do it again in the future. The same horse, if faced with a padlocked gate, would not usually jump over the gate (even 'top level' show jumping horses rarely jump out of enclosures) or indeed kick it down even though this behaviour would also lead to the same reward.

Just like all animals (including us) horses have evolved a form of intelligence that is necessary for their natural lifestyle. Therefore all animals have different kinds of intelligence.

The intelligence of a horse has evolved to enable it to survive as a large grazing herbivore that is hunted by predators.

The intelligence of horses is a subject that requires more research so that we can understand horses better. Many assumptions are made about the intelligence of horses especially as they tend to panic first and think later. For example, horses often do things that can seem remarkably stupid to us *usually* logical thinking humans. For example, if a rider falls from a horse but gets their foot caught in the stirrup, the horse does not reason that the rider cannot get free and therefore the best course of action would be to stand still. Instead the horse will instinctively panic at the unfamiliar sight and feel of the rider on the ground. The rider (hanging in this position from the horse by the stirrup) now looks and feels very much like a predator to the panicked horse. This fear is further reinforced if the horse runs away and kicks out at the 'predator' hanging from their belly but cannot dislodge this 'terrifying object'. Unless a horse has been trained otherwise *they will* panic and bolt in this situation.

No doubt though horses are sometimes equally perplexed by some of the strange things that we humans do!

It is very important that horse owners understand how the mind of a horse works in order to keep themselves and their horse safe. Learning more about how the mind of a horse works also has numerous benefits for the welfare of horses. It means that we then are more likely to see things from their perspective and understand that horses do not deliberately set out to annoy us or even harm us. Horses are just trying to get on with being horses in an often very confusing world!

Training effects

During all interactions with horses, it must be remembered that they are primarily '*fright* and *flight*' animals. Everything about horses, the way they are built and the way they behave, has evolved to meet this primary instinct. Other animals, including many herbivores, have evolved to defend themselves and their young if challenged. Horses have evolved to run first and defend themselves only if they cannot run away or cannot run fast enough. This is where the powerful backwards kick comes in, they can defend themselves while fleeing if necessary.

Horses are primarily fright and flight animals. They will always run away from danger given the choice rather than face it.

To a large extent horse training involves teaching the horse to *not* react instinctively but to respond to cues instead.

Horse training has evolved over many centuries. Some people like to follow 'traditional' methods and some prefer 'newer' methods. Whatever style of horse training you prefer it is important that you understand exactly what you are doing and think about how you train from the horse's perspective.

A large part of horse training is a combination of *habituation* (learning to become familiar with things) and learning to respond to cues (or 'aids' as they are usually called in the horse world). Even though horses are highly reactive and nervous (by necessity) they are very good at learning to accept familiar sights and sounds so that they can relax when in familiar and safe surroundings. This ability is a necessary behaviour for an animal that is naturally preyed upon; otherwise the animal would use too much energy being alert *all of the time* (even when there is no danger). This behaviour is part of the habituation process which horses respond well to (because it is already a part of their behavioural 'make up').

Good horse trainers use this process to train horses to 'become familiar' with all sorts of sights, sounds and experiences (stimuli). Think about police horses for example and what they learn to accept. Police horse trainers in particular use the process of habituation extensively when training.

Habituation, a good horse trainer knows how much 'pressure' to put on a horse, and when to remove that pressure.

Therefore a good trainer introduces a horse to 'scary' objects gradually and carefully. For example, they might ride a horse in an area that is near a road and get nearer to the traffic each day until the horse accepts traffic very close by. Teaching a horse in this way requires a lot of skill because if a trainer overestimates when a horse is ready to go to the next level of 'scariness' a horse can get frightened and panic. If the horse panics to the extent of running away (and the rider is not skilled enough to prevent this from happening) then the horse has actually learned that the best response is to run away (because running away took the horse away from the scary object), the opposite of what the trainer hoped to accomplish. For this reason it is important that people who train horses, and in fact have *anything* to do with horses, understand how easy it is to inadvertently teach a horse the *wrong* behaviours i.e. in this case to be more scared of things rather than 'become familiar' with them (habituated).

Horses can and do unintentionally habituate themselves to scary objects. For example, if a horse lives next to a busy road the horse will tend to habituate to the traffic over time (providing the horse has no previous bad experiences of traffic, otherwise the horse will simply get better at running away).

The free living ponies in The New Forest (UK) are totally habituated to traffic.

Habituation can work against a horse as well. For example, a horse that is thoroughly habituated to traffic would think nothing of walking down the middle of a busy road upon getting loose. In fact this happens when horses accidentally get out on to the roads and they are then a danger to themselves and people (due to the risk of collisions).

Horses are also able to *generalise* sights and sounds to some extent. The more they see and do the more they accept as 'normal'. Once they have learned to accept (been habituated to) a car moving past them they will also accept other cars that may be a different colour or different shape (as long as they are not *too* different). However if while riding a horse in a forest you come across an abandoned car that is upside down on the track in front of you do not be surprised if your horse is frightened. The horse has noticed two differences, the car is in the wrong place (the horse is not used to seeing a car in this environment) and the car is the wrong shape (the horse does not reason that an upside down car is still a car).

A horse can be habituated to traffic but there are usually some traffic situations that even a horse that is 'good in traffic' may still react to.

Even very well trained horses will revert to instinctive behaviour in some circumstances depending on their individual behavioural characteristics and their level of training etc. A well behaved, well trained horse can still react instinctively from time to time if subjected to 'too much, too soon'. For example, if a horse that is *usually* 'good in traffic' is subjected to a very large group of motorbikes sud denly passing close by at speed, the horse may still panic, because this level of 'stimuli' may be well beyond what the horse is currently familiar with (habituated to). Many horses can be trained to accept even this level of 'pressure', but while training, the increase in pressure needs to be very gradual.

Another example is that most horses habituate to the sight of various sizes and shapes of dogs, from small ones to large ones. Dogs are a very common sight and most horses have seen and accept a variety of dogs. However the sight of a large and extra hairy rare breed, such as an Afghan Hound, can frighten a horse not familiar with that breed, because the standard dog shape is different in this case (the flowing hair blurs the shape of the dog). Horses are *very* observant and notice many things that *you* may think are irrelevant.

Horses can habituate to almost any sight, including 'strange' looking (and strange moving) animals such as kangaroos!

At the same time, once a horse is taught to respond reliably to cues a rider or handler can steer a horse through an otherwise tricky situation because the reliable response to the cue overrides the horse's desire to panic. Hence the saying by some horse trainers that a well trained horse is always quiet, but a 'quiet' horse is not necessarily well trained. Or in other words, some horses may seem very quiet due to having a naturally good temperament but without proper training (so that the horse has reliable responses to cues) any horse will still panic if and when pushed out of its 'comfort zone'.

Horses have a very high *learning ability* and are able to learn certain tasks *very* quickly if trained properly. Not only does a horse learn quickly, but a horse will remember and respond to a cue indefinitely once the cue has been taught thoroughly (this of course includes 'bad' as well as 'good' responses). For example, a horse that has been thoroughly taught a certain 'movement' under saddle will still usually respond to the cue for that movement many years later even without practice in between.

It is now starting to be understood that horses do not necessarily need large numbers of repetitions once they have thoroughly learned certain tasks (yet many competition horses are 'trained' for hours at a time, practicing the same task over and over despite the fact that the horse can already perform the task well).

This is the sort of issue that the relatively new movement of **Equitation Science** investigates.

Horses have a very high learning ability and are able to learn certain tasks very quickly if trained properly.

If you are interacting with horses, be it riding or on the ground, you have the responsibility of learning about certain aspects of horse training. This is because *every time* you interact with a horse, you are consciously or unconsciously *training the horse*. If you do not understand what you are doing you may actually *train the horse to behave incorrectly*. In fact any professional horse trainer will tell you that after working on a particular horse's 'problem behaviour', they also need to work with the owner and change *their* behaviour. The most successful horse trainers are in fact good people trainers!

Horses are very good at learning what profits them (and therefore is worth doing again) and what does not profit them (and therefore should be avoided in the future). This behaviour keeps them relatively safe in their natural environment as an animal that is (was) preyed on by predators.

The science of **Learning Theory** is now being applied to horse training. Applying Learning Theory to your training regime reduces stress for horses *and* people. Learning Theory is not a training method in itself, it is a way of *examining and explaining how horses learn* and how this fits in with a particular training system. You can use this knowledge to examine your current training system and see if there are aspects of your training system that may be ambiguous to the horse. When you thoroughly understand *how horses learn* you can get the best from your chosen style of horse training. The above mentioned movement of **Equitation Science** examines how Learning Theory is best applied to horse training; see the list of **Recommended websites** in the **Further reading** section at the end of this book for a link to the International Society for Equitation Science's (ISES) website.

Most forms of horse training (and indeed domestic animal and captive animal training) use **negative reinforcement**. In a training context 'reinforcement' means that it increases the likelihood of that behaviour reoccurring. More recently many horse trainers are also using **positive reinforcement**. All good horse trainers, however they label their own training method, already use negative reinforcement, even if they do not use the scientific term to describe it. Many of them call it 'pressure and release' training or similar. However, many trainers confuse the term negative reinforcement with the term **punishment**, thinking that they are the same thing, but they are very different.

Think of *negative* reinforcement as the *removal* of something (such as lead rope pressure) and *positive* reinforcement as the *addition* of something (such as a scratch in a favourite place or a food reward). *Punishment* is also the addition of something (such as the

47

creation of fear or pain) but it occurs at a different time (see below). In the following simple and common scenario, i.e. loading a horse into a trailer, you can see how the three approaches could be applied.

To load a horse into a trailer you put pressure on the lead rope until the horse steps forward (***negative reinforcement***). Once the horse steps forward the pressure on the lead rope is removed. Remember, if it helps, think of the term negative in the same way that it is used in mathematics, negative means to take away. If the horse has previously been *thoroughly* taught to lead (presuming the pressure is applied and removed at the correct time) the horse will load in to the trailer. Hence the saying among many horse trainers that if a horse will not load in to a trailer you do not have a loading problem, you have a leading problem!

A common example of negative reinforcement is when a rider removes their leg pressure as the horse moves forward.

If the horse will not move from pressure on the lead rope then you may need to apply gentle but regular taps with a stick to the body of the horse whilst maintaining the pressure on the lead rope. Again, as soon as the horse takes a step forward (even if it is not all the way into the trailer) the pressure (in this case the taps *and* the pressure on the lead rope) are removed. Negative reinforcement is being used because you *take away* the pressure when the horse responds correctly. Therefore negative reinforcement starts *before* the response (it creates the response) and stops when the horse responds correctly. Negative reinforcement says 'yes' to the horse.

A definition of **punishment** in the above scenario would be that if the horse did not move forward, or the horse jumped sideways rather than moved forward when given the cue (pressure from the lead rope or taps to the body plus pressure on the lead rope), then the handler might hit the horse with the stick, yank on the lead rope or yell etc. Punishment occurs *after* the wrong response is given (even if the response is that the horse does nothing). Punishment says 'no' to the horse. But it does not tell the horse what is required. The horse only learns that certain situations should be avoided in the future.

The problem with punishment is that if the horse does not understand the cue or is already fearful then it makes the situation worse not better. Punishment usually occurs when the emotional level of the handler has increased to frustration or anger, which in turn increases the emotional level of the horse (pain, fear and confusion). Whereas negative reinforcement is applied without emotion, or in a logical sequence, in order to create the desired response.

If you were to use **positive reinforcement** in this scenario of loading a horse onto a trailer, you would scratch the horse in a favourite spot or give the horse a food reward *after* the horse has responded correctly (i.e. stepped forward, usually due to negative reinforcement being first applied). Again using the mathematics analogy, positive is adding something (the reward). Positive reinforcement is applied *after* the response. If you were to reward the horse *before* the correct response then this is not positive reinforcement. For example, if the horse refuses to move forward and you give him or her some food anyway. You could in fact call this bribery and it does not work because the horse will have been rewarded for the *wrong* behaviour (i.e. not moving forward). As with negative reinforcement the timing of positive reinforcement is crucial. Indeed it is a *lack* of good timing by a handler or rider that creates the wrong behaviour in a horse, because they are inadvertently *rewarding the wrong behaviour.*

Positive reinforcement (reward based training) is used to teach horses many things from tricks to improved work under saddle.

Dog trainers now use positive reinforcement extensively, and as mentioned before, many horse trainers are now adding this training tool to their repertoire of techniques. More research is required about this subject in order to fully understand its benefits and any possible shortcomings.

Negative reinforcement and positive reinforcement are very powerful training tools when applied correctly. However punishment that may involve the infliction of pain is *not*, as it does not communicate to the horse what you want him or her to do. As mentioned before, punishment says no rather than yes, and it can frighten the horse. Punishment can actually undo your training as the horse becomes afraid to try responses. A horse learns by trial and error, but if the horse becomes afraid to try then it becomes fearful and stressed. Eventually some horses give up trying and *learned helplessness* can be the result.

Learned helplessness is where the subject (in this case the horse) becomes fearful of trying responses because in the past they have been punished for trying. When the horse cannot work out a way of not being punished they may decide to do nothing, because trying leads to punishment. Dull 'switched off' behaviour is the result. A horse in this state may even appear to not feel pain or any other stimuli, leading an uninformed handler or rider to label the horse as 'lazy' or 'ignorant' or as having other undesirable traits.

Learned helplessness in horses also occurs outside training, for example when a horse is kept alone. A horse kept alone has two possible responses, the horse can remain in a highly anxious state which uses up lots of physical and emotional energy, or can develop 'learned helplessness'. This is an emotional state which uses up less energy but is still stressful. Because a horse gives no visible (to the inexperienced horse person anyway) or aural signs of stress it is assumed that the horse is 'happy' to be alone.

A last word about training: by training a horse you replace many of the horse's instinctive reactions (such as panicking about situations, being dangerous to ride etc.) with 'learned responses' (such as being calm in potentially scary situations and being good to ride etc.). In so many ways this results in a horse that is a pleasure to be around (and a less stressed horse). However always remember that a well trained horse will do *what you ask, for as long as you ask* (because the horse now has *totally* reliable responses to a set of given cues) so it is *your* responsibility to only ask the horse to do what is reasonable. An inexperienced horse rider/handler/owner, thinking that a horse is compliant simply because the horse 'wants to please' for example, can seriously overwork a horse without realising that the horse is trained to such a level that only sheer exhaustion would cause that horse to stop working.

*This is only a very brief introduction to the subject of training.
There are some exciting developments in the horse world on this
subject. You owe it to your horse and yourself to learn about these.
Training is a fascinating subject and what you learn about
training will help you in many ways (not just with horses). See the
Further reading section at the end of this book.*

Time-budgets of horses

The way that domestic horses spend their time when not being handled/ridden/trained is a very large part of their day and actually affects how horses behave overall. For example, a horse that is stressed due to inappropriate living conditions may also be difficult to handle, ride and train due to that stress affecting their behaviour. Understanding what horses do (or should do) with their time is essential for good horse management. Good horse management is essential if you are to have a safe, sound and healthy horse.

A horse that is stressed due to inappropriate living conditions (in this case a horse that is anxious due to being separated from other horses) may also be difficult to handle, ride and train.

Many animals have been studied in their natural environments to discover what the 'time-budget' is for that particular species. The term 'time-budget' means the amount of time animals spend doing what is necessary throughout each day and night to maintain themselves.

Not surprisingly animals that catch and eat other animals, predators (carnivores and omnivores) and animals that are prey (animals that are caught and eaten) differ in the amount of time that they spend carrying out daily maintenance activities.

The time-budget of most predators involves short periods of high activity (to catch and eat prey) and long periods of inactivity (drowsing and sleeping), to digest the high calorie/high protein food (meat) that they have eaten. Dogs (omnivores) and cats (carnivores) are predators. Notice how many hours your pet dog or cat sleeps when you are not actually interacting with them. Horses (herbivores) are very different.

Herbivores eat plants and have many different behaviours to carnivores and omnivores because they have to be alert most of the time (watching and listening for predators). In addition they have to eat for a much larger part of each day because their food is relatively low in calories and takes a long time to collect and chew. Horses have one of the longest daily grazing periods of all the plant eating herbivores because they do not ruminate (regurgitate and re-chew their food). As horses chew their food only once they have to do it very thoroughly. Once swallowed the food can generally only be further broken down by the various micro-organisms in the gut, so the better the food is chewed *before* swallowing the better the micro-organisms can do their job. The horse digests food in the hindgut *while* grazing. This means that a horse spends most of the day and night 'on the hoof', grazing, ready to flee if necessary.

Studies have shown that the time-budget of adult wild/feral horses comprises:

- Grazing, between 12-20 hours a day.
- Sleeping, between 2-6 hours a day.
- Loafing, between 2-6 hours a day.

Time spent grazing

When horses are living in relatively natural conditions the time spent grazing is usually spread throughout the day and night with the most intensive grazing periods tending to be at dawn and dusk. A grazing bout is usually around three hours long and bouts of sleeping and loafing are interspersed among these grazing bouts. The *total* time spent grazing each day depends on the quality of the grass/plants that are available. On better quality/more abundant feed a horse will spend less time grazing (between 12 and 16 hours) and more time loafing and sleeping (however this will still result in a very obese horse if the grass is high in energy). During hard times, such as during a drought or a harsh winter, a horse will increase their grazing time up to as much as 20 hours a day (if any plants are available). Horses will eat leaves, twigs and almost anything fibrous, including poisonous plants, if there is nothing else to eat. During these times loafing behaviour (social behaviour) becomes of lower priority and the horse spends all available hours foraging and sleeping.

Understanding how horses spend their time is important in terms of their management. Horses have a very different time-budget to us and other predators such as cats and dogs for example.

Daily behaviour time-budget

The ability to increase their grazing time when necessary is a factor that makes horses such a successful feral animal in tough and varied climates around the world. When the going gets tough a horse simply increases the amount of time spent eating and therefore increases the amount of food eaten if any food is available. Even though this food may be very low quality, as it would be in times of drought or cold harsh weather, it still means that the horse usually manages to survive because of this increased volume. This strategy makes horses more successful in tough conditions than cattle for example because cattle simply run out of hours in the day (because they have to chew their food twice) when their feed source becomes more fibrous/lower in quality.

Grazing takes up the largest part of a horse's day. In fact a horse should spend more time grazing than carrying out all of the other behaviours put together.

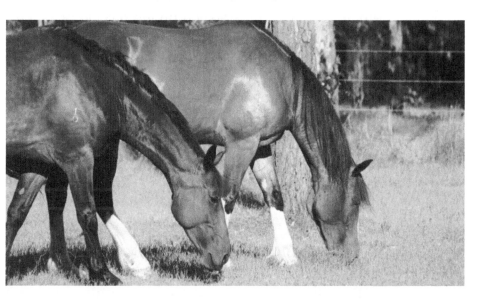

Interestingly if a horse is removed from pasture for a few hours (a management tactic often carried out by owners with the intention of reducing an overweight and/or laminitis prone horse's intake) the horse will condense their grazing time into the period when they are turned out again (increasing their bite and chew rate at the same time). So for example if a horse is confined to a yard or stable for several hours and then turned out again it will not make much, if any, difference to their total intake for the day!

Time spent sleeping

Adult horses usually sleep/doze for a total of about 4 hours per 24 hours (young horses sleep for longer). These four hours are divided roughly into totals of two hours spent sleeping lying down and two hours spent dozing standing up.

Like grazing, sleeping takes place in bouts. A sleeping bout is around 15 minutes at a time and is interspersed with grazing and loafing bouts. For example, a horse might sleep lying down for 15 minutes and then graze some more and so on.

Horses have various sleeping/dozing positions. Lying flat out on the side with the head and neck outstretched, lying down but resting on the sternum (with the nose resting on the ground or with the head up off the ground) or a third position involves the horse dozing standing up. A horse uses what is termed 'the stay apparatus' to lock the joints of the legs in place, and can even do this while resting a hind leg when nodding off in the standing position.

In this picture the various positions can be seen. The horse on the left was dozing standing but has become alert to the photographer. The next horse is flat out and asleep, while the other two are on their sternum, the first has woken and the second is asleep.

Horses use a lot of energy when sleeping flat out on their side due to having large lungs. Lying down rests the legs but the large lungs (and other organs) have to work harder when a horse is stretched out flat. This is why a horse often makes a groaning noise when fully prone, as breathing is quite an effort in this position. However this sleeping position is very necessary as it is thought to be the only position that a horse can achieve deep (REM, rapid eye movement) sleep.

As horses age they find getting down and up again from the ground more difficult. Eventually they may stop lying down altogether because they have learned that it is too difficult to get back up again. To a horse, being able to get up from the ground quickly is a safety factor. Innately horses know that they have to be able to rise quickly and run from danger. Be aware of this with old (especially if arthritic) horses because they may not be getting enough (or any) deep sleep due to having stiff sore joints therefore this can become a welfare issue. This is one of the factors that should help you to make a decision about if and when to euthanise an old horse.

Standing up again after lying down requires a lot of strength and energy. Older horses can reach a stage where they struggle to get back up again after lying down and so they become unwilling to lay down at all and therefore can suffer sleep deprivation.

In a group of horses one horse usually stays standing when the others are asleep on the ground. The standing horse is more alert than the others (even if dozing) while the others sleep more deeply. This is a good example of how herds operate. Horses that live alone do not get to benefit from this system of shared responsibility. Some nervous horses are even unwilling to lie down frequently enough when on their own as they have no other horse to watch over them as they sleep. These horses can suffer from sleep deprivation as they are unwilling to spend enough or any time sleeping in the fully recumbent position.

Time spent loafing

The term 'loafing' encompasses all the other behaviours that horses carry out during the day and night. Loafing includes activities such as mutual grooming (allo-grooming) and playing. Loafing also includes simply standing around together, especially in the shade when it is hot, nose to tail. They use their tails to keep flies off each other (a form of 'you scratch my back and I'll scratch yours' behaviour). In cold wet weather horses will stand in a sheltered spot together because their large bodies help to keep each other warm.

Standing around together is very important to horses. Horses will ignore other comforts to be able to stand next to each other. This is demonstrated when horses are kept separately in 'private paddocks' where they will often ignore shade/shelter in order to stand next to each other on either side of the fence.

Typical loafing behaviour for horses involves just standing around together in the shade.

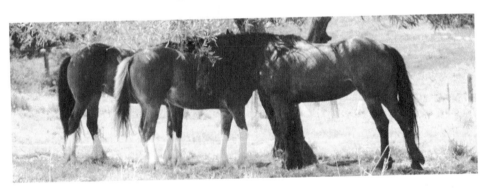

Mutual grooming involves two horses approaching each other and using their incisor teeth to 'groom' each other (another example of a mutually beneficial behaviour). Mutual grooming is a *very* important behaviour for horses. Areas that they cannot reach with their own teeth can be scratched by the other horse. It is also a way of maintaining bonds among herd members. Studies have shown that during bouts of mutual grooming the heart rate of a horse is significantly lowered.

Mutual grooming is yet another very important behaviour to horses. It forms part of their skin care regime!

Playing is also very important to horses of all ages. In young horses, play is an opportunity to learn and practice the skills required for adult life. Younger horses spend more time than older horses playing but all horses naturally play even into old age if they are able (in contrast to many other large grazing herbivores). Horses will play with other horses, in the case of domestic horses, geldings play together as if they are wild colts. Horses will also play with objects (such as sticks and in the domestic situation they will play with other objects such as road cones, 'horse balls' etc.). A herd of normal healthy horses will get excited and tend to run around at certain times such as when turned out into a new pasture or when the sun comes out after a period of rain. Sometimes no excuse is required and horses will gallop 'just for the fun of it'. When horses are deprived of the company of other horses they are deprived of the opportunity to play with other horses.

This active behaviour is partly due to the fact that horses (in a natural situation) have to be ready to flee from a predator instantly. The first line of defence for a horse is to run (whereas cattle will defend themselves and their young, thus the horns on their head) therefore horses 'practise' fleeing as part of their natural behaviour.

Understanding the time-budget of horses is important for the welfare of horses. Horses are highly social grazing animals and these facts should not be ignored, yet often are. By looking at the physiology, behaviour and time-budget of natural living horses we can see that a horse should spend a minimum of 12 hours a day just chewing food and should be allowed to interact with other horses in order to carry out important social activities.

Herd and social behaviour

Horses are meant to live in herds and normal horses are never alone by choice. These facts drive the behaviour of horses and cause them to do some of the things that can seem irrational to us, such as panic if they get separated from other horses. Management systems do not usually take these important facts about horse behaviour into consideration and when coupled with a diet that is too low in fibre, some horses develop stereotypical behaviours such as 'cribbing' and 'weaving' (see the section **Abnormal horse behaviour**).

We all know that horses are herd animals (even people who have nothing to do with horses tend to know this fact) but many people do not completely understand what this entails. A fuller understanding of equine herd and social behaviour means that modern horse management systems can be designed to incorporate rather than ignore these basic but very important facts about horses.

Wild and feral equines naturally live in herds (see the section **Natural living horses**). Horses are naturally highly social animals. When horses live in a herd situation they have a rich and varied social life that includes activities such as sexual behaviour, play behaviour and mutual grooming behaviour. Actual fights are rare in established groups with threats or gestures being more common. Horses that live in herds get to exercise their senses frequently. They smell each other when greeting and they smell each others dung (in order to gather 'information' about each other). They use their highly developed senses of scent and taste while grazing to help with plant selection. They use their equally highly developed visual and auditory senses to look out and listen for danger. Touch is very important to horses and mutual grooming bouts are frequent. Horses have a very strong fundamental instinct to form attachments to other horses. These attachments are often for life.

Horses that live in a herd communicate with one another mainly by using body language that consists of subtle signals (see the section **Body language**). An extensive body language system is necessary in any animal species that lives in a group. This behaviour is one of the reasons why herd or pack animals are much easier to train than animals that are solitary by nature (because they are used to noticing and responding to the behaviour of other members of the group).

Horses, if allowed, will form bonds that last for life.

Living as part of a herd also has other advantages such as 'safety in numbers'. Grazing involves having the head down in the grass, which reduces visibility. More sets of eyes and ears means that predators can be seen or heard sooner. A horse living alone in the wild would be much more likely to be caught by a predator. This horse would also expend too much nervous energy by having to stay in a permanently alert state. Horses that live in herds can take it in turns to be alert and to rest and therefore the responsibility of keeping a lookout is shared among herd members.

Actual aggression is not common in free-living horses; more often than not horses display body language that seeks to *avoid* aggression. This is because aggression is dangerous for the aggressor as well as the victim. Horses have many facial expressions and gestures that convey their intentions to other horses so that actual aggression needs only to be used when necessary.

Horses that live in captivity can be more aggressive than wild/feral horses if the way they are managed leads to this. In captivity horses are often fed high energy supplementary feed (concentrates) which leads to feeding competition. We tend to initiate aggression when we feed concentrates to horses that are turned out together. In the wild, grass is generally available to all the horses or none of them at any particular time. Their food source is spread far and wide and so they do not have to fight to get it. In the wild no one comes along with a bucket of high energy feed to create this aggression. Horses should ideally be separated into individual yards or stables for the short time that it takes to eat any concentrate feed both for their safety and the safety of handlers.

Settled herds of domestic horses tend to be more passive if the group members are reasonably constant. A group which has constantly changing members (because horses are being removed or added to the herd) will tend to be less secure.

When horses live in captivity their strong herd instincts do not disappear and cannot be disregarded. When living in a herd situation domesticated horses interact with one another in much the same way that they would in a wild/feral situation. Domestic horses have retained all of their herd instincts and this is one reason why domestic horses can and do survive successfully if they are released or escape into the wild.

Grazing and feeding behaviour

Food is very important to horses because in the natural situation grazing and browsing takes up more time than all of their other behaviours put together (including sleeping) (see the section *Time budgets of horses*). Horses spend a *lot* of time grazing and browsing. Grass is their main staple although they will eat other plants including certain bushes and trees. Horses will even eat berries and other fruits if they get the chance. It has been found that free-living horses eat a very large variety of plants on a daily basis. It is therefore important that you aim to have a variety of species in your pasture and to ensure that your pasture is not a monoculture (a monoculture is where there is only one species of plant in a given area). A good pasture for horses contains plants such as legumes, herbs, sedges etc. as well as several species of grass (for more information see the *Further reading* section).

Chewing is important for the production of saliva that buffers acid in the stomach (and helps to keep stomach ulcers at bay, see the section *What horses are...*). While chewing a horse is relaxed. Conversely, a horse that becomes alert stops chewing. This is because chewing is noisy and it is only by stopping chewing that the horse can hear properly.

The head of a horse is in a lowered position when eating plants (as opposed to eating out of a raised feeder for example). The joints and soft tissues of the horse's head and neck have evolved so that the head can comfortably be kept low for hours at a time (interspersed with occasional periods of lifting the head to look around).

This lowered head position also serves another function, to drain the airways. The lungs of a horse are large and delicate and whenever the head of a horse is lowered the airways are draining debris down the nose, helping to keep the lungs clean.

Horses are highly selective grazers. They are able to be much more selective than cows for example because their prehensile (highly flexible) top lip allows them to sort what they want from what they do not want as they graze. They also have two sets of incisors which meet and are very sharp. The sharp paired incisors of horses allow them to bite plants down to ground level. Horses, if left on a pasture for too long, will continuously select plants that they like and graze them to the ground, leaving the rest to grow long and rank. The long rank areas are also where they drop their dung (see the section **Dunging behaviour**). The types of plants that horses prefer eventually become grazed out unless particularly hardy.

Chewing is important for the production of saliva. While chewing a horse is in a relaxed state.

Horses have no concept of 'leaving some for another day' or any other pasture management strategies that would result in more grass in the future. If grass is available horses will eat it, even if they make themselves incredibly fat in the process or if they completely eat out their favoured species.

Deliberate overeating in horses is due to an innate need that drives them to eat more than is needed when food is available and to store it as body fat. Most mammals have developed this strategy to get them through hard times. The type of food available to *free living* horses means that this increase in body fat is usually reasonably gradual. Then, when feed is not so readily available (such as during a harsh winter or drought), these reserves of body fat can be utilised for survival.

In an ideal year, wild/feral horses will enter winter slightly over-weight, lose condition over the winter (as they use up those body fat reserves) and enter spring slightly underweight, when the rich high sugar grasses start to re-grow. This seasonal weight fluctuation is rarely seen in domestic horses and this can have health implications particularly in regard to obesity and laminitis.

In the domestic situation a horse will *still* attempt to put on weight whenever possible (because this is an innate need) but of course a domestic horse does not take into account that the food available is usually much higher in energy than what would be available in the free-living situation, and that a responsible horse owner will not see them starve in the winter or during a drought! Domestic horses must be regularly monitored for increases and decreases in condition. As a horse owner you need to be aware of what is a dangerous level of weight increase because this can lead to life threatening conditions such as laminitis. At the same time you need to be aware of what constitutes reasonable weight loss (see the **Further reading** section for some recommended reading on the subject of feeding horses).

As horses have evolved to eat for many hours at a time they have huge muscles in the jaw which enable chewing for hour after hour. When you are feeding your horse remember that they are meant to eat large amounts of low energy fibrous food (the equivalent of vegetables and salad to us), not small amounts (or even worse, large amounts) of high energy food (the equivalent of 'junk food' to us). Low energy fibrous food takes a long time to chew and digest and keeps a horse occupied (and fulfils the chewing need) for hours at a time.

While a horse is grazing they are also walking (because the plants are stationary the horse has to keep moving in order to graze them). A horse generally only bites each plant once before selecting another plant (if the pasture is healthy, not too short and is bio diverse). It is estimated that a horse takes 10,000 steps a day while grazing! This slow steady movement is vital for horse health. The circulatory system of a horse depends on this movement to keep blood and lymphatic fluid moving around the body. Not to mention the many other benefits of exercise. Horses that are kept mainly confined miss out on the numerous benefits of grazing.

Horses have huge muscles in the jaw that enable them to chew for hour after hour. As they chew they produce and swallow copious amounts of saliva. If horses do not get enough fibre to chew they can end up with gastric ulcers due to insufficient amounts of saliva reaching the stomach.

Modern day horse management has resulted in many horses being over confined, under worked and fed meals that are too high in energy but too low in fibre. These types of feed are eaten much more quickly (due to being more energy dense) and this results in long periods of time where the horse has nothing to do. An additional problem is that modern grasses are largely developed for the cattle and sheep industries with these grasses increasingly being bred to be higher in sugar and starch as this is what farmers need and want for milk or meat production. In most countries (those that have temperate rather than tropical climates) 'improved' ryegrass has become the number one grass of choice for farmers. Horse owners need to be very aware that for sedentary modern horses (and most of them fall into this category) this grass is far too high in energy. A study has shown that large numbers (possibly over 50%) of domestic horses in the UK for example are obese. The same study showed that most owners tended to *underestimate* the condition score of their overweight horses by at least one point (on the condition scoring scale). The subject of obesity in domestic horses is becoming a major welfare issue.

If horses cannot graze for whatever reason they should be fed on ad-lib low sugar/low starch hay if possible. Keep in mind that domestic horses are usually happy to share hay and grass, but not concentrates. So separate areas are needed if and when feeding concentrates.

Incorrect feed types and amounts can cause problems, either behavioural (see the section **Abnormal horse behaviour**), physiological or both. Some of the most important physiological problems that can occur when horses are fed incorrectly are colic, gastric ulcers, laminitis and insulin resistance (similar to diabetes in h mans). Laminitis can occur when horses are eating too much high sugar/high starch grass or being fed too many concentrates, but not enough low energy fibre. Try to keep in mind with horses (even overweight ones) that you should *not* be aiming to feed *less* food but that you should be aiming to feed food that is *lower* in calories (the equivalent of less chocolate and more salad to us). Starving even a fat horse is cruel and counterproductive. An additional factor for horses that are overweight is often that the horse is not receiving enough exercise.

A domestic horse should be fed a diet that is as close to natural as possible. Either grazing on high fibre/low sugar/low starch pasture or being fed on forage made from these plants. Fibrous low energy pasture and hay take a long time to eat and digest and therefore occupy a horse for much longer and keeps the gut functioning as it should, reducing the incidence of behavioural problems and health problems such as colic, gastric ulcers, laminitis and other obesity related disorders.

Paddock/field behaviour

Horses can cause a lot of wear and tear to land and this is due to combination of factors. Poor land management is common in th horse world; also horses are large active animals. Horses that ar being fed supplementary feed will stand at a gateway (sometime even if there is plenty of grass available) and wait, long before fee time, causing problems such as bare areas (and therefor mud/dust) and soil compaction near a gateway.

Horses will also create paths between a water trough and a fa vourite loafing spot or between a shelter and water. Separate horses will walk the fence lines to try and get to other horses or w stand in a particular area if that is a point where they can be near c see another horse. Separated horses will play over fences which dangerous behaviour (fence injuries are very high on the list of ser ous injuries to horses).

Healthy horses will regularly canter or gallop when turned ou This is normal behaviour for a horse. Horses are naturally muc more active animals than cattle for example (who defend first an run second). Remember, horses are primarily flight animals, so a mentioned earlier, running around is actually practising this beha iour. This active behaviour is also dependant on how much they ar confined before being turned out, how fit they are and how muc energy they are receiving from supplementary feed etc.

In a natural situation horses are free to move to another area, or out of the sun or rain, to higher ground when it is wet, towarc other horses (or away from them) etc. if and when they choose.

Domestic horses stand around, sometimes for hours at a tim mainly because fences prevent them from being able to mov themselves to where they want/need to be. It is possible to redres some of these issues with domestic horses. The use of good gra ing management systems will reduce or eliminate the effects these behaviours on your land while keeping horses healthy ar happy, a win-win situation. See the *Further reading* section at th end of this book.

Horses will spend many hours standing at a gate waiting to be taken to feed or for feed to be brought to them.

Dunging behaviour

When domestic horses graze a pasture they tend to dung and urinate in some areas (the 'roughs') and graze in others (the 'lawns'). They are the only grazing animal to do this. In contrast cows and sheep are not as rigid as to where they drop dung in a pasture. All grazing animals, horses included, will not eat around or near their own species dung (thought to be a natural parasite ('worm') prevention strategy).

These rough areas of a paddock/field tend to increase in size over time because geldings and mares face in to the centre of a rough to drop manure. Stallions back into it and have a tendency to create a neat pile of manure, this behaviour is scent marking behaviour so that any other stallions in the area know they are there. The way that mares and geldings drop dung leads to increasingly larger roughs over time. In the roughs the plants become long and rank and the areas may also become dominated by weeds (especially the types of weeds that thrive on high levels of nutrients). At the same time the decreasingly smaller lawns become overgrazed. Without intervention more and more of the pasture becomes unavailable for grazing over time.

If left to their own devices horses dung in some areas of a paddock (roughs) and graze in others (lawns). Note the long, untouched rank grass. Careful pasture management and the utilisation of good grazing management systems will reduce or eliminate the effects of this dunging behaviour while at the same time keeping your horses healthy and happy.

Pastures that have marked areas of roughs and lawns are often termed 'horse sick'. There can be many more times the number of infective parasite larvae in roughs than lawns. The whole pasture ends up with an imbalance of nutrients as horses take from the lawns (by grazing) and deposit (urine and manure) in the roughs. Horse urine and manure is high in nitrogen, potassium and phosphorus, therefore the roughs receive lots of nutrients from manure and the lawns do not. In addition 'horse sick' land is unsightly and gives the general public a poor impression of horsekeeping.

In a free-living situation wild/feral horses are not forced to graze over their own manure due to the space that they have available to them. Also, in the wild many different species of animal graze the same areas, each grazing near and around each other's manure

72

and taking in each other's parasites ('worms') which kills the parasites. Most parasitic 'worms' are generally 'host specific' meaning that they can only survive when picked up by the host animal with which they have evolved. As equines are not at all related to ruminants (cows, sheep, goats, alpacas etc.) their parasites have evolved quite separately whereas certain ruminant parasites can infect other ruminant animals (for example, some of the parasites of sheep can also infect alpacas) because the host animals are more closely related.

So dunging behaviour is something that has to be managed in the domestic situation otherwise horses will increase their parasitic 'worm' burden' and render a pasture 'horse sick'. Chemicals such as 'worm pastes' (anthelmintics) cannot be totally relied upon to control worms (although they are necessary) because this is leading to various other problems (for horses *and* the environment) therefore we must adopt good pasture management and pasture maintenance strategies to use in conjunction with the use of anthelmintics (for more information see the **Further reading** section at the end of this book).

Horses create areas called roughs (where they also drop dung) and graze in other areas (called lawns). This behaviour results in uneven grazing, weeds and wastage. Good pasture management is needed to reduce or eliminate the effects of this behaviour. Pasture management is a very important part of horse ownership because unhealthy land leads to unhealthy horses.

Sexual differences

There are some differences in behaviour between male and female horses; however this does not tend to be as extreme a difference as many people believe, especially between geldings (castrated male horses) and mares.

It is generally believed that geldings are the most tractable of the three groups of horses (mares, geldings, stallions) however, as with most situations, there are often exceptions. Some geldings still exhibit some sexual behaviour particularly in springtime when hormones levels are rising (due to an increase in energy derived from pasture, longer day length etc.). Many geldings show no interest in mares, but some show a lot of interest to the extent that they will mount mares and will also act aggressively with other geldings that are in the area. This behaviour can be the result of being incorrectly or incompletely gelded (usually due to one testicle not descending properly, called a 'rig' or more correctly a cryptorchid) or in some rare cases the horse *is* correctly gelded but is still able to secrete the hormones that cause him to behave like a stallion (without being fertile). An equine veterinarian can help to determine the situation.

The behaviour of mares varies from mare to mare. A small number of mares show a distinctive change in behaviour when they are 'in season' (are ovulating). Many mares however show very few if any behavioural changes. Unfortunately the term 'moody mares' has become more commonplace in modern times, partly because commercial supplements have been developed for this largely supposed 'condition' therefore it has led to mares being labelled as 'moody' for the slightest of behavioural changes. Many mares in fact actually become 'friendlier' when they are in season. Signs that a mare is in season include frequent urinating, lifting the tail, squatting the back end and standing with the hind legs spread when stallions or geldings are around.

A mare with a foal may be protective of the foal (especially in the first few days after giving birth) and a mare can become aggressive if she feels she has to defend the foal (although many mares are not particularly protective at all). In the wild a mare will run away from any threats (and expect the foal to follow) but in captivity she cannot always do this. Mares and foals can become very agitated if they are separated from each other to the extent that they can run through or jump over whatever is in the way in order to get back together.

A mare with a new foal can sometimes be protective but often they are not. In the wild mares only defend their foal if trapped, their first choice is to run and the foal is expected to keep up. Foals are usually able to keep up with their mother within hours of being born!

Domesticated stallions range in their behaviour from being equally as tractable as a well trained mare or gelding, to being 'difficult' to manage. Unruly behaviour is usually due to a lack of understanding, poor handling and training. In the domestic situation stallions are often kept separately from other horses. When a stallion is kept alone he will tend to 'walk the fence line' in an attempt to be with mares.

It is a miserable existence for a stallion to live alone because horses are herd animals and are intensely social and thrive in the company of other horses. Domestic stallions *can* be kept with other horses, especially if they have always lived with other horses and have not lost their 'socialisation skills'. For example, a stallion can live with a single mare or a group of mares if these mares are to be put in foal to him anyway. A domestic stallion may even be able to live with other males as part of a 'bachelor group'. Remember stallions in the wild/feral situation either have their own herd/harem of mares or are part of a bachelor group, they are *never* alone by choice.

Stallions should not be owned/kept by inexperienced horse people. It is not fair to expect a stallion to 'put up with' the handling abilities of someone who is still learning. Even though an educated stallion can be as well behaved as any other horse it is also not fair to keep a stallion unless you plan to breed with him. Again breeding should only be carried out by professional horse people because there are *far* too many unwanted horses in the world already, even professional horse people breed far too many horses. Visit a 'low end' horse market and see the number of unwanted horses, ponies and donkeys that end up going to a knackery. This problem is not the fault of the knackeries and *is entirely* the problem of people who breed unwanted animals. This problem is further compounded when a lack of good handling/training renders these animals of even lower value.

When keeping domestic horses in a herd you need to understand and acknowledge their sexual differences and you may need to make alterations to the group mix in some cases. Generally speaking a group that consists of a gelding and several mares usually works well (because this is similar to a free-living 'family' group, even though the male of the group is a gelding), whereas more geldings than mares in a group can lead to some fighting between the geldings. This is only a generalization, each group is different just as each horse is different and it is up to you to observe the group and make changes if necessary. See the section ***Introducing a new horse to an established herd.***

There are some differences between the sexes of horses that should be acknowledged and accounted for however there are many inflated myths about these differences i.e. that stallions are always 'difficult' to manage, that mares are always 'moody' and that geldings are always the most tractable of the three. Keep in mind that a well trained horse is a well trained horse and will behave appropriately in any reasonable situation if handled properly.

Individual differences

Even though all horses have the same basic behavioural characteristics they also have individual differences. Some are more reactive than others and some are quicker to adapt to new situations than others. Individual differences between horses can be due to one or a combination of several factors such as natural differences in temperament, age, different 'life experiences' and different training experiences etc. Horses (just like any animal, including us) also differ from their siblings, even when they have the same sire and dam and the same 'upbringing'.

Age can account for some differences but horses can remain 'difficult to manage' even into old age if they are not trained properly.

A lot of emphasis is put on breed differences in domestic horses. Some breeds are regarded as quieter than others. Selective breeding for good temperament (rather than speed or beauty for example) has led to some breeds being *generally* quieter than others; however this is not a hard and fast rule. Not all *breeders* select breeding stock for temperament, a horse that has a good temperament *as well* as an attractive look is worth a lot of money. Unfortunately many breeders can only afford stock that has one trait or the other. Compounding this fact is that a breeder *can* win show classes with a beautiful horse that has a dubious temperament. This is because good training and handling can, to a large extent, cover up the fact that the horse does not have a good temperament *and* some judges are willing to overlook poor behaviour if they particularly like the look of a certain horse. On the other hand a breeder will *not* win classes with a horse that is ordinary to look at, no matter how good the temperament! Horses that are 'successful' in the show ring tend to be the ones sought after for breeding. Therefore it can be dangerous to believe that a horse will be quiet just because it is a certain breed or has won certain show classes. Keep in mind that there are huge variations of temperament within, as well as between, breeds.

Thoroughbreds that are fresh 'off the track' are not suitable for *inexperienced* people to handle or ride, but this is not necessarily simply a breed difference (Thoroughbreds have been selectively bred to be able to run very fast) but is also due to a combination of factors such as fitness, age (they tend to be still young when retired from racing) and the fact that they have just come out of training to gallop as fast as possible. All of their previous training has been focused on 'going' rather than 'stopping'. Conversely they may have been habituated to many sights and sounds during their career and appear relaxed in certain situations. Standardbreds (trotters and pacers) are also racehorses and are also often available for sale after finishing their racing career. There are organisations that responsibly re-home ex-racehorses which you should consider contacting before taking on a Thoroughbred or Standardbred 'off the track'.

Generally 'hot blooded' horses such as Thoroughbreds and Arabs are thought to be more sensitive and excitable than 'cold blooded' horses such as draught breeds (i.e. Clydesdales), however, as before, there are many exceptions. 'Hot blooded' is a term to describe horse types that evolved in hotter climates and have thinner skin and are of a lighter build. 'Cold bloods' originate from colder climates and have thicker skin and a heavier body type (i.e. Clydesdales and Shires). 'Warmbloods' are a mixture of the two types (although they are now also regarded as a breed in their own right).

It is better to regard every horse as an individual. Each horse has had its own set of influences and there is no such thing as an automatically reliable, well behaved horse just because it is this or that breed or a certain age (or indeed a certain colour!). A well trained horse will appear 'quiet' and 'well behaved' in most situations; this does not mean that those traits will be passed on if this horse is used for breeding. Training a horse to such a level (especially if the horse was 'difficult' to start with) takes many hundreds, sometimes thousands, of hours.

Abnormal horse behaviour

Domestic horses become stressed if they are not allowed to carry out certain normal behaviours. For example, playing, mutual grooming and grazing are all part of their normal range of behaviours. Abnormal behaviours come about when a horse is stressed due to being prevented from carrying out these natural social and grazing behaviours.

Animals in captivity (domesticated animals) are less stressed if important facts about their physiology and behaviour are taken into account when designing and implementing management systems for them. Most modern zoos in the western world have taken these facts on board and go to great lengths to 'enrich' the 'lifestyle' of any animals in their care by providing better (and usually bigger) enclosures and more natural feeding experiences for them. Unfortunately in the horse world many horses are still being kept using outdated management systems that *do not* take natural horse behaviour and physiology into account and would actually be regarded as unacceptable practices by a modern zoo!

Many stables in use today would not pass muster in a modern zoo! In this picture the stable 'door' is a floor to ceiling cage front preventing the horse from putting its head over the door. The walls between each stable are solid from floor to ceiling.

There are certain behavioural problems ('called stereotypical behaviours') associated with stress in domesticated horses. Stereotypical behaviours are defined as repetitive, invariant behaviour patterns with no obvious goal or function. Stereotypical behaviours are not seen in animals in the wild and are understood to be abnormal and are therefore a negative factor in the management of animals in captivity. Stereotypical behaviours can occur in all animals, including humans (compulsive hand washing is one example of such behaviour in humans). In horses they take various forms and the most common ones are:

- Fence-walking. Repeatedly walking backwards and forwards along a fence line.

- Weaving. Repeatedly rocking from one front leg to the other in a stable or at a gate, some horses will also do this when traveling.

- Crib-biting. Grasping an object (an old fashioned name for a horse's feed manger is a crib) with the front teeth (incisors) and swallowing.

- Wind-sucking. Arching the neck and swallowing without grasping an object.

- Box-walking. Repeatedly pacing around and around the stable.

Wind suckers will commonly grab hold of any convenient surface, in this case a fence.

- Wall-kicking. Repeatedly kicking the walls of a stable, usually with one or both back feet, even to the point of making themselves sore/lame.

- Self-mutilation. Swinging the head to repeatedly bite themselves. This behaviour is typically carried out by stallions.

Free-living horses do not exhibit these stereotypical behaviours because they are not subjected to the same stresses as domestic horses, have a natural diet *and* have a complex and varied 'lifestyle'.

In the horse world stereotypical behaviours are inaccurately and unfortunately termed 'vices'. The usual response to these 'vices' is to put a horse that displays them under even more stress by trying to prevent the horse from carrying out these behaviours (by using wind-sucking collars and anti-weaving bars for example). The assumption is that the horse is misbehaving and has to be restrained or punished, rather than recognising that the horse is simply reacting to stress.

Crib-biting collars and other preventative measures do nothing about the cause of stereotypical behaviours. Prevention is not the answer as it simply increases the stress levels.

Oral stereotypical behaviours such as crib-biting and wind-sucking can arise because the horse does not have access to enough fibre. When horses chew they also produce and swallow saliva in copious amounts (see the section **What horses are...**). Research has shown that horses that crib-bite and wind-suck are actually swallowing saliva to relieve pain in the stomach (which buffers the acid in the stomach). It used to be thought that they were swallowing air (hence the term 'wind-sucking'). Other stereotypical behaviours such as weaving and box/fence-walking are due to frustration at not being able to move enough or move towards where they want to be (usually to be near other horses).

There are many outdated myths connected with stereotypical behaviours, for example it is commonly believed that if a horse watches another horse performing a stereotypical behaviour they will learn to do it. This is not true as horses do not learn in this way once they are adults (this is called observational learning). If more than one horse is exhibiting a stereotypical behaviour in a given area it is more likely to be because both or all of the horses are living in conditions that *cause* these stereotypical behaviours. Isolating horses because of this belief will simply lead to an increase in stress and an increase in the behaviour.

Much of the information that is readily available to horse owners (i.e. in magazines, on the Internet etc.) on the subject of stereotypical behaviours is archaic and even cruel. This information usually concentrates on prevention only and does nothing to reduce the stress levels of the horse in question, in fact they usually vastly increase stress levels for the horse. There are also many products on the market that physically prevent horses from carrying out stereotypical behaviours and these products (such as crib-biting/wind sucking collars) again do not treat the cause of the problem and can in fact increase the stress. The stereotypical behaviour is the horse's way of coping with the stress and gadgets which stop the horse from carrying out this behaviour simply mask the symptoms. This suppressed behaviour may then manifest in a different abnormal behaviour, learned helplessness or aggression.

Imagine visiting a zoo and observing animals wearing preventative devices of some kind. You would not be happy about the situation and would probably complain yet in many stables you will see various preventative devices such as crib-biting/wind-sucking collars and weaving bars commonly being used. A relatively new invention is an electric collar for horses that crib-bite and wind-suck! This collar delivers a small electric shock to the horse if the horse attempts to tense the muscles in the throat area (a prerequisite for cribbing/sucking). Such a device would *never* be allowed in a zoo where the animals are on public display because the public would find it totally unacceptable.

Once a horse has developed the habit of performing a certain stereotypical behaviour it will usually carry on performing the behaviour for the rest of its life, even if the reason the horse was stressed in the first place is removed. The behaviour may be seen much less however over time and allowing the horse to perform the behaviour (rather than trying to prevent the behaviour), while at the same time improving the 'lifestyle' of the horse, is usually the best solution.

The subject of stereotypical behaviours in horses is complex and suggestions for further reading are recommended in the **Further reading** section.

If your horse performs a stereotypical behaviour try to think of ways that you can improve their 'lifestyle' rather than aim to simply prevent your horse from carrying out the behaviour. Remember, prevention will usually increase the level of stress in the horse. This does nothing to make the behaviour disappear and in fact will usually make the behaviour more likely to occur (once the preventative device has been removed). This is why horses that wear a 'cribbing/sucking' collar usually begin to crib/suck immediately that the collar is removed, which makes their owner feel justified for using it.

Improving the 'lifestyle' of domestic horses

The previous sections in this book have been about free-living (wild/feral) horses and their behaviour. This information has been compared to information about domestic horses so that you understand firstly what horses really are and what is important to them and secondly, how the 'lifestyle' of domestic horses is often very different to that of their free-living relatives.

In this age of enlightenment more and more people are willing to improve the 'lifestyle' of their horse, both for the welfare benefits *and* the improvement in performance that results from a healthier and arguably happier horse. They just need practical information about how they can do this in their situation, hopefully the following information will give you lots of helpful suggestions.

All horses have basic requirements that must be met in order to thrive both physically and mentally. Animal welfare agencies talk about 'the five freedoms' of animals. These are the five *basic* rights that *all* animals should have. Translated into horse parlance these are:

- **Freedom from thirst and hunger.** A horse should have ready access to fresh, clean water and sufficient amounts of the correct foodstuffs. Horse feeding practices must take into account their requirements for a very high fibre diet as that is what they have evolved to eat.

- **Freedom from discomfort.** A horse should have an appropriate environment. Adequate space and shade/shelter are important. Management systems must take into account normal horse behaviours. Horses are herd animals and are inherently social and require company. It is time to rethink outdated traditional management practices.

- **Freedom from pain, injury and disease.** A horse owner or carer must know at least the basics of horse care and be able to recognise when a horse needs veterinary attention or is in need of a horse dentist or farrier or other horse health professional.

- **Freedom to express normal behaviour.** A horse owner or carer should understand horse behaviour. This knowledge is important not only to provide suitable living conditions for any horses in their care but also to train them humanely. Understanding horse behaviour is also essential for a rider or handler's safety.

All horses should be free to express normal behaviours such as running around with other horses.

- **Freedom from fear and distress.** A horse owner or carer should not place a horse in a situation where the horse continues to suffer stress/distress. Nor should a horse owner or carer use training methods that cause fear, pain or distress. By using humane training methods horses can be trained effectively and safely.

Always remember that your horse is a horse (of course) and allow him or her to live like one whenever possible. All horses benefit from:

- **An increase in time spent grazing**. All horses should be allowed to graze as much as possible. There is no better feed for a horse if the grass is high fibre/low sugar/starch. If the grasses are 'improved' (i.e. high sugar/starch grasses developed for cattle) then careful management will be required to make sure that their sugar/starch intake is not too high.

- **An increase of fibre in the diet**. If you do not have enough available grazing (or the grasses are inappropriate for horses) then feed as much hay as possible. Select high fibre/low sugar/low starch hay and feed it 'ad-lib' (free choice, available 24/7). This means that the horse spends more time chewing and swallowing saliva which is what a horse is meant to do.

Feeding ad-lib hay and allowing horses to live together goes a long way to improving their 'lifestyle'.

- **An increase in movement**. Create an environment which enables and encourages more movement. Movement is so important to a horse, millions of years of evolution have resulted in a grazing athlete that thrives on movement. When you take on horse ownership remember that horses are meant to move, a lot! Increasing movement for your horses may mean a change of management system. Read about ***The Equicentral System*** that we advocate which increases movement in horses while at the same time allows better land management, a win-win situation (see ***Our other publications*** at the end of this book).

- **A reduction in time spent in confinement**. All horses need time each day to move round outside, with other horses. Stables are often no better than cages and prevent horses from even touching each other. Make sure that horses are only stabled/confined when necessary. Many horse owners feel that their horse actually 'likes' their stable. One of the reasons that horses can appear to enjoy being stabled is because horses are usually keen to get into their stable after they have been turned out for a while. This is because a stable usually contains their feed so the horse is being positively reinforced each and every time they are led into the stable. Once the feed has been eaten the horse is usually just as keen to leave the stable but by now the door is closed and the horse is fastened in for the night etc.

Stabling horses is often a 'necessary evil' for many horse owners because they do not have much choice if they do not own their own horse property. In this case aim to make sure your horse spends at least some time outside each day, preferably in the company of other horses. Even if pasture turn out is not available (because of the season etc.) your horse should still be able to be turned out onto a surfaced area for example (with other horses). If you own your own horse property and already have stables established consider changing them to a more 'horse friendly' design. This could mean making a row of stables into an open fronted 'run in barn' etc. If you are building stables from scratch consider leaving part of the stable wall open above chest height so that the horses can interact with each other.

- **An increase in the time spent in contact with other horses at pasture**. *Actually with another horse, not just on the other side of the fence from one.* Allowing horses to interact over a fence is usually far more dangerous than putting them in the same area together due to the risk of fence injuries. Increasingly many horse owners keep horses in separate areas believing this to be the safest method of horse management. Many owners do not want to risk injuries to their horse and this is why they prevent them from coming into contact with other horses. Horse play is rough although not usually as rough as it appears to us humans. All animals, including humans, use play as a form of development and to strengthen bonds. This is an important part of the socialisation of a horse and research is being carried out into how important herd living is in terms of a horse's learning development. The strong instinct that horses have to be together means that separated horses will 'walk the fence' or even go through or over a fence/gate to be with another horse. The resultant fence injuries are usually far worse than anything that horses do to each other when kept together. Even horses that appear to be low in the social structure will still choose to stay with other horses rather than be alone. In fact two horses can seem to have a strong dislike for each other (to us humans) but if separated they may become frantic. So aim to keep your horse/s in a herd.

If you are building stables aim to make them as horse friendly as possible. These particular stables allow interaction as well as provide an area for each horse to eat in peace.

- **An increase in the amount of time spent behaving like a *real* horse**. If you are aware that your horse lives in relatively stressful conditions aim to let your horse have regular 'time-out' sessions. During these times let your horse go without rugs, get muddy, interact with other horses etc. Even very valuable (in monetary terms) horses can and should be allowed access to other horses. Quiet, unshod smaller horses make great companions for large dressage horses for example (make sure they are introduced safely and properly, see the next section). Think of it as R and R time. You would not like to go without your holidays, friends and general relaxation time so don't expect your horse to. Keep reminding yourself that winning competitions may be *your* goal but it is not the goal of your large hairy herbivore no matter how hard you try to convince yourself! A more relaxed 'happier' horse will ultimately be sounder, stronger, safer, healthier etc. so it will all be worthwhile in the end.

- **An increase in opportunities to make their own decisions**. This might not sound like such an important factor (although after reading this book hopefully, if you did not already see it this way, you will now also see this as an important factor). Domestic horses kept in traditional systems are not able to make many, if any, decisions in their day to day life. For some horses, literally every step they take is governed by a human (in the case of a fully stabled horse that is only 'exercised' while being trained in an arena for example). By changing the management system horses can be *allowed to make choices*, such as where they want to stand (in the shade or out in the sun etc.), which other horses they spend time with etc. This is a *huge deal* for a horse. The **Equicentral System** that we advocate allows horses to make their own decisions as much as possible. (See **Our other publications** at the end of this book).

*See the **Further reading** section at the end of this book for recommendations of where you can find more information about all of the above suggestions for improving the 'lifestyle' of your horse.*

Introducing a new horse to an established herd

Careful introduction of a horse into a herd will vastly reduce any risks and an added bonus is that pasture management is much easier when horses live together because they can be rotated around areas as a group. One horse per paddock/field does not allow the pasture any rest and recuperation time, a welfare issue for grass! In fact 'managing' pasture in this way leads to stressed grass that is not good for horses *and* land degradation problems (we cover this subject in detail in our two books about pasture, see **Our other publications** at the end of this book).

If you decide to integrate your horses into a herd because of the horse welfare and land management benefits there are several things to think about and steps to take so that the integration goes smoothly. First of all think about each of the horses in question and decide if it will be best to have one herd or more than one herd. To end up with just one herd is the best outcome because this will be much easier for land management but this may not be possible in your situation.

Some of the factors that will help you to decide include the age and sex of the individual animals. For example, young and boisterous horses may be too energetic for a very old horse. On the other hand, older horses are usually very good at holding their own with younger horses up until a certain age (which is different for all horses) when they may start to need more specialised care in general.

It generally works best if there are more mares than geldings in a herd because some geldings still have some entire (stallion) behaviour and can become protective of mares to the point that they will chase other geldings if mares are present. So if you decide to have two herds for example it may be better in this case to have one gelding with the mares in one herd and the rest of the geldings in another herd. This is similar to the natural groups that occur in the wild/free-living situation i.e. a stallion with some mares and a bachelor group consisting of males of all ages. All horses are different though and various scenarios can work.

There are many ways that a new horse can be introduced to a group of horses. Remember that the existing group will have a social structure and the introduction of a new member will disrupt this. It is not safe to simply turn the new member out into the group and 'let them get on with it'. In a confined space the new horse can be run into or over a fence by the other horses. It is better to let the new horse get to know at least one member of the group in separate securely fenced yards (preferably 'post and rail') or stables that have an area where two horses can safely interact with each other. This way the newcomer can approach the fence or wall to greet the other horse but can also get away if necessary. There will usually be squealing but this is perfectly normal behaviour when horses meet and greet each other.

Careful introduction of new herd members will reduce the chances of injury.

When these two horses are accustomed to each other you can turn them out together and then add other herd members gradually one at a time. Try not to give them any hard feed (if the horses are being supplementary fed), only hay, just before you turn them out so that they get down to grazing sooner. It is safer if the horses are left unshod at least for the initial introductions. Hoof boots can be used also. Make sure that resources are plentiful and easy to reach, for example, situate the water away from a corner so that they can each drink safely and no one gets trapped. The group must be watched very carefully during these times.

Keep in mind that you will usually see the most excitable behaviour between the horses in the first hour or so after turning them out together.

Good horsekeeping involves acknowledging what is important to a horse. It also means acknowledging that you have a responsibility to provide all the basic needs and requirements to keep any horses in your care physically and mentally healthy.

Remember: A horse is a horse of course!

Final thoughts

Thank you for reading this book. We sincerely hope that you have enjoyed it. Please consider leaving a review of this book at the place you bought it from, or contacting us with feedback, stuart@equiculture.com.au so that others may benefit from your reading experience.

Further reading

Our other publications

Buying a horse property

Horse pasture management

Understanding horses and pasture

Horse property planning

Manure, water and vegetation on a horse property

Riding arenas and training yards

Stables, yards and shelters

Horse property fences and gates

Horse properties - a management guide

These books cover the sustainable management of a horse property. Several of them cover The Equicentral System that we recommend. See our websites for more information about these books.

www.equiculture.com.au and www.horseridersmechanic.com

Our latest books are:

Horse Rider's Mechanic Workbook 1: Your Position and

Horse Rider's Mechanic Workbook 2: Your Balance

You can read the beginning of each of these books (for free) on the Horse Rider's Mechanic Website (**www.horseridersmechanic.com**).

Most of our books are available in various formats including paperback, as a PDF download and Kindle. You can find out more on our websites:

www.equiculture.com.au and **www.horseridersmechanic.com**

New books are becoming available all the time, make sure you sign up for our mailing list while you are on our websites so that you find out when they are published. You will also find out about our workshops and clinics while on the websites.

Other recommended books

Equine Behavior Paul McGreevy (2004) Saunders, Sydney, Australia.

Equine Behaviour: Principles and Practice Mills D & Nankervis K (1999) Blackwell Science, London.

Equine Welfare Marthe Kiley-Worthington (1998) J. A. Allen & Co. London.

Horse Behaviour Waring GH (1983) Noyes Publications, New Jersey.

The Behaviour of Horses in Relation to Management and Training Marthe Kiley-Worthington (1983). Reprinted 1999.

The Behaviour of the Horse Fraser AF (1992) Cab International, UK.

The Domestic Horse: The Evolution, Development and Management of its Behaviour (2005) Daniel Mills and Sue McDonald (ed) Cambridge University Press.

The Horse's Mind Lucy Rees (1984) Stanley Paul. UK. Currently out of print.

The Nature of Horses Steven Budiansky (1998) Orion Books Ltd, London.

The Truth about Horses : A Guide to Understanding and Training Your Horse Andrew McLean (2003) www.aebc.com.au.

The Welfare of Horses, Animal Welfare Notes Series Book 1 Dr Natalie Waran (ed), Springer Books, Dordrecht, Netherlands, (2007).

Recommended websites

Our websites www.equiculture.com.au and **www.horseridersmechanic.com** have extensive information about horsekeeping, horse care and welfare, riding and training.

The International Society for Equitation Science (ISES) looks at applying science (in particular Learning Theory) to the subject of horse training. Holds an international conference every year. **www.equitationscience.com**

The Equine Behaviour Forum has been on the go for many years and has lots of great information, articles etc. It has an international following and is well worth joining **www.equinebehaviourforum.org.uk**

Marthe Kiley-Worthington, scientist and author of books about horse behaviour and welfare. Now runs an Eco Farm and Research Centre in France **www.eco-etho-recherche.com**

Equilibre, a Spanish web site with some great behaviour and training articles (many in English) **www.equilibregaiasp.wordpress.com**

Bibliography of scientific papers

Bertone, J.J. (2005) Excessive drowsiness secondary to recumbent sleep deprivation in two horses. The Veterinary clinics of North America. Equine practice 22(1):157-62.

Hampson, B.A., De Laat, M.A., Mills, P.C. & Pollitt, C.C. (2010) Distances travelled by feral horses in 'outback' Australia. Equine Veterinary Journal Special Issue: Proceedings of the 8th International Conference on Equine Exercise Physiology Volume 42, Issue Supplement s38, pages 582–586, November 2010.

Hampson, B.A., Morton, J.M., Mills, P.C., Trotter, M.G., Lamb, D.W., & Pollitt, C.C., (2010) Monitoring distances travelled by horses using GPS tracking collars. Australian Veterinary Journal Volume 88, Issue 5, pages 176–181, May 2010.

Harris, P.A. (1999). How understanding the digestive process can help minimize digestive disturbance due to diet and feeding practices, In: Harris, P.A., Gomarsall, G.M., Davidson H.P.B., Green, R.E. (Eds.), proceedings of the BEVA Specialist Days on Behaviour and Nutrition. Newmarket, Equine Veterinary Journal 45-49.

Ince, J., Longland, A., Newbold, C.J. & Harris, P. (2011) Changes in proportions of dry matter intakes by ponies with access to pasture and haylage for 3 and 20 hours per day respectively for six weeks. J Equine Veterinary Science Volume 31,

Issues 5-6, May-June 2011, Page 283 Proceedings of the 2011 Equine Society Symposium.

Longland, A., Harris, P. & Barfoot, C. (2011) The effect of wearing a grazing muzzle vs not wearing a grazing muzzle on pasture dry matter intake by ponies. J Equine Veterinary Science Volume 31, Issues 5-6, May-June 2011, Pages 282 283 Proceedings of the 2011 Equine Society Symposium.

McGreevy, P.D., Cripps, P.J., French, N.P., Green, L.E. & Nicol, C.J. (1995). Management factors associated with stereotypic and redirected behaviour in the Thoroughbred horse. Equine Veterinary Journal 27: 86-91.

McGreevy, P.D., Richardson, J.D., Christine, J.N. & Lane, J.G. (1995). Radiographic and endoscopic study of horses performing an oral based stereotypy. Equine Vet. J. 27, 92.–95.

McGreevy, P.D.,French, N.P. & Nicol, C.J. (1995). The prevalence of abnormal behaviours in dressage, eventing and endurance horses in relation to stabling. Vet. Rec. 137, 36–37.

McGreevy, P.D., Webster, A.J.F., Nicol, C.J., 2001. A study of the behaviour, digestive efficiency and gut transit times of crib-biting horses. Vet. Rec. 148, 592 596.

Menard, C., Duncan, P., Fleurance, G., Georges, J-Y. & Lila, M. (2002). Comparative foraging and nutrition of horses and cattle in European wetlands. Journal of Applied Ecology. (39). 120-133.

Nicol, C. J.; Davidson, H. P. D.; Harris, P. A.; Waters, A. J. & Wilson, A. D. (2002). Study of crib-biting and gastric inflammation and ulceration in young horses. Veterinary Record 151 (22): 658–62.

Stephenson, H.M., Green, M.J. & Freeman S.L. (2011) Prevalence of obesity in a population of horses in the UK. Veterinary Record 168-131 vetrecc6281 Published Online First: 17 January 2011.